The Law of Christ:
A Theological Proposal

A. Blake White

Also By

A. Blake White

_____

The Newness of the New Covenant

The Law of Christ:
A Theological Proposal

A. Blake White

5317 Wye Creek Drive, Frederick, MD 21703-6938
phone: 301-473-8781 or 800-376-4146 fax: 240-206-0373
email: info@newcovenantmedia.com
Website: www.newcovenantmedia.com

The Law of Christ: A Theological Proposal

Copyright 2010 © by A. Blake White.

Published by: New Covenant Media
                       5317 Wye Creek Drive
                       Frederick, Maryland 21703-6938

Orders: www.newcovenantmedia.com

Printed in the United States of America

ISBN 13: 978-1-928965-33-6

To Alicia,
Thanks for all you are to me.

e;nnomoj Cristou/

TABLE OF CONTENTS

FOREWORD

I have one real problem with Blake White's book, *The Law of Christ: A Theologcal Proposal.* It should have been written thirty years ago. The first chapter is titled, *"Justification: The Starting Point of Christian Ethics."* Martyn Lloyd-Jones would have said a loud "Amen" to that. In his excellent book on *"Spiritual Depression,"* Lloyd-Jones starts his book with a chapter on justification. He insists nearly every problem in the Christian life grows out of a failure to understand the true nature of justification. Blake White says, "The doctrine of justification, primarily found in Paul's letters, has rightly been considered the heart of the gospel itself" (p. 13).

White is familiar with both history and the current theological scene.

> Recently the traditional protestant understanding of justification has come under immense attack from several circles, even within "evangelicalism." This section of the book will show that justification in Paul is being vindicated in the divine courtroom at the final judgment, grounded in the death and resurrection of Christ, located in union with the Messiah, and obtained by saving faith alone. Grasping this reality is the important starting point for ethics. It is what sets the Christian faith apart from all other religions (p.14).

White's book strikes a powerful blow at the silly notion that you can separate true biblical holy living from correct biblical theology.

> Faith is the exclusive means for salvation in Christ. However, it is not faith in and of itself that saves however;

rather Christ saves through faith. Neither is it a mere "faith in faith," but saving faith is always a Christ-centered faith. This is important to stress in our day where a vague notion of faith is gaining popularity. Biblical faith has a definite content to it.

Concerning faith and obedience, the Reformation motto has rightly been that we are justified by faith alone, but faith is never alone. Faith and obedience are distinct but absolutely inseparable (see James 2:14-26). Paul introduces and closes the book of Romans writing that he is seeking to bring about the obedience which flows from faith among all the nations (Rom. 1:5, 16:26). In the new creation, which has been inaugurated by Christ's resurrection, faith works through love (Gal. 5:6, 6:15). Paul also speaks of the work of faith (1 Thess. 1:3; 2 Thess. 1:11). Faith *always* goes public in acts of obedience. In Martin Luther's words, "Oh, it is a living, busy, active, mighty thing, this faith; and so it is impossible for it not to do good works incessantly. It does not ask whether there are good works to do; but before the question arises, it has already done them, and is always at the doing of them. He who does not these works is a faithless man." A mere assent that does not express itself in works is false faith. Tom Schreiner writes, "Faith inevitably manifests itself in obedience, so that faith is the seed and works are the fruit." Faith is the root, and obedience is the necessary fruit (p. 36ff).

One of the characteristics of this book is the clear balance. The chapter on the *indicative*, meaning the fact of what God has done for his people in Christ, and *imperative*, meaning what God now commands and expects from his people, is excellent.

It is vital to the Christian life to keep these in balance. The imperative always flows out of the indicative. The indicative always expresses itself in the imperative....If one over-emphasizes the need for obedience and neglects the good news of what God has done for us in Christ (namely justification, the divine declaration), there is a tendency towards legalism…On the other hand, if one over-emphasizes the good news of what has taken place in Christ and does not call people to obedience, they will become worldly and immoral, not taking God's commands seriously enough…This relationship is really what sets Christianity against all other religions. Pastor Tim Keller writes, "Religion operates on the principle 'I obey—therefore I am accepted by God.' But the operating principle of the gospel is 'I am accepted by God through what Christ has done—therefore I obey" (p. 43).

The book is divided into two parts. Part 1 is "Foundations," and the second part is "The Law of Christ." Some will be disappointed with the second section, and others will be elated. When both the far left and far right are upset, it is usually a good sign. Those desiring a "new covenant absolute list" of laws that take the place of the tablets of stone will be disappointed. Those insisting Paul's theology of "not under the law" means *I am a law unto myself and am free to do as I please* will also be disappointed. Some will say, "White is not a true new covenant theologian."[1] Others will accuse him of being a legalist, and still others will cry "antinomian." I predict the book will help many of God's sheep to understand much better the path their Shepherd would have them take in their daily living.

The law of Christ cannot be reduced to a list of do's and don'ts. It certainly involves specific things that can be "listed" as right or wrong, but it is far more than a list like

---

[1] I have yet to discover what a "true new covenant theologian" is.

the ten words written on stone. The law of Christ is love, but it is also the example of Christ. Everything Christ taught is part of His law, but so is everything His apostles taught a vital part of his law. Christ himself is his law personified. The whole of Scripture, as interpreted through the lens of Christ as the new covenant prophet, priest, and king, is a part of the law of Christ. These things are exegetically established in chapters 4–11.

Chapters 12 and 13 deal with the vexing problem of continuity and discontinuity. Many theologians insist that the law of Christ and the law that God gave Moses is the same law. All they see is continuity. This idea is, of course, essential to their system of theology of law. If the "moral" law of Christ differs from the "moral" law that God gave Moses (the Ten Commandments), then we have two different canons of conduct and that destroys the "one covenant, one redeemed people, and one unchanging 'moral' law" thesis. John Murray's book on ethics, _Principles of Conduct_, was written for the specific purpose of proving there is only one unchanging canon of conduct, the Ten Commandments, for all men in all ages. White proves conclusively that the law of Christ is far more than the law that God gave to Moses at Sinai. The Ten Commandments, given as the "words of the covenant" (Exodus 34:27, 28), are done away in Christ.

However, White's next chapter shows there is some definite continuity. The law and the prophets are applicable to new covenant believers interpreted in light of Christ. White quotes Doug Moo approvingly:

> "The law remains authoritative for the disciple of Jesus only insofar as it is taken up into his own teaching," "Law,"

in *DJG*, 461. Elsewhere he writes, "The *whole* law, every 'jot and tittle,' is fulfilled in Christ and can only be understood and applied in light of that fulfillment," in "The Law of Moses or the Law of Christ" (p. 145)

He also quotes Jason Meyer:

"The coming of Christ has caused a paradigm shift that calls for recalibrating all former commands in the light of His centrality. This approach recognizes that the law of Moses in its entirety has come to an end in the sense that the believer does not start by asking, 'What did the law teach?' The believer begins at the point where his Christian life began: Christ. The believer found new life in Christ and so now comes to Christ to find out how to live out his new life." (p. 145).

Perhaps this is the place to mention one of the great strengths of White's book. There are 337 footnotes from a wide range of authors. These quotations are extremely well chosen and clearly illustrate the point being discussed. These notes alone are worth the price of the book. You will be amazed at the number and caliber of men quoted. Although it would be very wrong to call any of these men "new covenant theologians" since only one has so identified himself, however, it is true to say that many of the quotations show that the particular writer is in full agreement with the particular new covenant theology point that White is stressing at the time.

The book closes with a chapter on natural law. The last paragraph gives a good summary.

This natural law is eternally normative, as it reflects the will and character of God. It consists of transcendent moral principles. We are only bound to those parts of the Mosaic law which are part of natural law, which is repeated in the law of Christ. As Luther puts it, "We will regard Moses as a teacher, but we will not regard him as our lawgiver—unless he agrees with both the New Testament and the natural law....we are not to follow [Moses] except so far as he agrees with the natural law. Moses is a teacher and a doctor of the Jews. We have our own master, Christ, and he has set before us what we are to know, do, and leave undone" (p. 150ff)

Today there are books and articles by the dozen both defending and condemning new covenant theology. This is not "just another one" to add to the list. This book is unique. Blake White not only understands the problems involved in his subject; he articulates clear biblical answers. Whether you agree or disagree with his answers, a careful reading of this book will give you a better understanding of what Paul means when he speaks of the "law of Christ."

John G. Reisinger
February 8, 2010

PART I – FOUNDATIONS

INTRODUCTION

What are Christians to obey? The Bible is the simple answer of course, but upon further investigation, things aren't quite that simple. For example, I am sure we have all heard a Christian condemning and calling homosexuality an abomination based upon Leviticus 18:22 or 20:13. However, if one looks on the next page at Leviticus 19:27, should we not also conclude that we shouldn't get haircuts or shave? Why is one normative, but not the other? So it turns out the question of Christian ethics, or rules of conduct is quite complex. To ask what a Christian should or should not do is a Biblical Theology question.[2] It is a hermeneutical question.[3] The issue of continuity and discontinuity has plagued theologians and exegetes from the earliest days of the church. In some ways, the whole

---

[2] Brian Rosner defines Biblical Theology as "theological interpretation of Scripture in and for the church. It proceeds with historical and literary sensitivity and seeks to analyse and synthesize the Bible's teaching about God and his relations to the world on its own terms, maintaining sight of the Bible's overarching narrative and Christocentric focus," in "Biblical Theology," in *New Dictionary of Biblical Theology,* ed. T. Desmond Alexander, et al. (Downers Grove, IL: InterVarsity Press, 2000), 10.

[3] Michael Hill, in his helpful ethics book, *The How and Why of Love: An Introduction to Evangelical Ethics* (: Matthias Media, 2002), notes that "Only a proper understanding of the whole Bible will answer the question about the validity and application of the moral elements of the Law...the hermeneutic determines the ethic...Biblical ethics starts with doing biblical theology," 45, 54, 247.

book of Acts is dealing with this very subject. Jonathan Edwards wrote, "There is perhaps no part of divinity attended with so much intricacy, and wherein orthodox divines do so much differ, as the stating of the precise agreement and difference between the two dispensations of Moses and of Christ."[4] Similarly, John Wesley wrote, "Perhaps there are few subjects within the whole compass of religion so little understood as this."[5] The task requires the care of the master of a house, "who brings out of his treasure what is new and what is old" (Matt 13:52). The wise scribe rightly puts the canon together.[6] We need to

---

[4] Jonathan Edwards, "An Humble Inquiry," in *The Works of Jonathan Edwards Vol. 1*, (Peabody, MA: Hendrickson Publishers, 2003), 465.

[5] From his 1749 sermon, "The Original Nature, Property, and Use of the Law," quoted in David A. Dorsey, "The Law of Moses and the Christian: A Compromise," *Journal of the Evangelical Theological Society* 34, no. 3 (September 1991): 321. Douglas Moo says, "Few issues are of greater significance to biblical theology and , ultimately , to systematic theology as the relation between the Testaments," in "The Law of Moses or the Law of Christ," in John S. Feinberg, ed., *Continuity and Discontinuity: Perspectives on the Relationship Between the Old and New Testaments* (Wheaton, IL: Crossway Books, 1988). The contemporary theologian Richard Lints agrees, writing, "I suspect that almost all major controversies in evangelical theology could be reduced in the end to a difference concerning the relationship of the Testaments," in *The Fabric of Theology: A prolegomenon to Evangelical Theology* (Grand Rapids, MI: Eerdmans, 1993), 301 n.13. There are three primary theological systems that put the canon together differently. This work is from a new covenant theology perspective, as I believe this system does the best job of letting biblical theology inform systematic theology.

[6] Thomas R. Schreiner writes, "The wise scribe in the kingdom is like the householder who rightly assembles both new and old and relates the old to the new (Matt. 13:52) insofar as it relates to the

acknowledge that we are in the deep end of the theological swimming pool and must proceed with care and humility. The issue of continuity and discontinuity is such an important issue because one's conclusions on this issue will influence one's view of justification, sanctification, and indeed one's entire theological outlook. This book will come from a New Covenant Theology perspective.

Before entering the discussion of what it is Christians are to do, it is important to lay the theological foundation for Christian ethics. Christianity, after all, is not simply a code of ethics. It is not just a moral system. Being a Christian is not simply trying to "do what Jesus did." No, the foundation of the Christian life is the gospel of Jesus Christ. All else flows from the good news of Christ crucified for sinners. As Michael Horton writes, "It is the Good News that yields good works. Salvation is not the prize for our obedience but the source."[7] This being the case, we need to make sure we understand how we are made right with God before we investigate how we are to live. Add to that the fact that the doctrine of justification, which answers the question of our standing before God, is being downplayed and misunderstood in our day. To that precious Reformation truth we now turn our attention.

---

kingdom of God. The wise scribe, in other words, does not merely repeat the old but rather explains how the old relates to the new and is fulfilled in the new, so that the old does not retain precisely the same status now that the new has arrived," *New Testament Theology* (Grand Rapids: Baker Academic, 2008), 625.

[7] Michael Horton, *The Gospel-Driven Life* (Grand Rapids: Baker Books, 2009), 155.

CHAPTER 1

JUSTIFICATION:
THE STARTING POINT OF
CHRISTIAN ETHICS

Before turning to ethics, or how Christians should live, it is important to note that how we live does not fundamentally determine our status before God. The gospel is an announcement *outside of us*, first and foremost. It is good *news*. News is a particular kind of communication that comes to us from the outside.[8] The doctrine of justification, primarily found in Paul's letters, has rightly been considered the heart of the gospel itself. In Romans 1:16-17, Paul introduces the theme of the letter by saying he is not ashamed of the *gospel*, for in it the *righteousness*[9] of God is revealed. Paul introduces his letter to the Galatians by warning his hearers not to accept a false *gospel* (1:6-9). In Galatians 3:8-9, he writes that the Scripture, foreseeing that God would *justify* the Gentiles, preached the *gospel* beforehand to Abraham. Justification has been called the article of the standing or falling church

---

[8] Idem, *Christless Christianity* (Grand Rapids: Baker Books, 2008), 104.

[9] It is important to note that our English words "righteousness" and "justify" have the same Greek root "*dikai-*." See Stephen Westerholm, *Perspectives Old and New on Paul: The "Lutheran" Paul and His Critics* (Grand Rapids: Eerdmans, 2004), 262-63.

(Luther), the hinge upon which all religion turns (Calvin)[10], and the atlas upholding the entire Christian faith (Packer).[11] Recently the traditional protestant understanding of justification has come under immense attack from several circles, even within "evangelicalism." This section of the book will show that justification in Paul is being vindicated in the divine courtroom at the final judgment, grounded in the death and resurrection of Christ, located in union with the Messiah, and obtained by saving faith alone. Grasping this reality is the important starting point for ethics. It is what sets the Christian faith apart from all other religions.

The Current Debate

The doctrine of justification in Paul is hotly debated today. Much of this debate stems from the so-called "new perspective on Paul." It is more correct to say new perspective(s) on Paul because there are major differences in each of the scholars sympathetic to the new perspective.[12] This brief section will survey the general

---

[10] Calvin, _Institutes of the Christian Religion_ 3.11.1, ed. John T. McNeill, trans. Ford Lewis Battles, Library of Christian Classics, vols. 20-21 (Philadelphia: Westminster, 1960; Reissued, Louisville, KY: Westminster John Knox Press, 2006), 726.

[11] R.C Sproul, _Getting the Gospel Right: The Tie That Binds Evangelicals Together_ (Grand Rapids: Baker Books, 1998), 83.

[12] This will be the briefest of surveys, but today, the written material on this issue is voluminous. The best resource to date is Stephen Westerholm, _Perspectives Old and New on Paul: The "Lutheran" Paul and His Critics_. Also see the short but insightful Donald A. Hagner, "Paul & Judaism," in _Revisiting Paul's Doctrine of Justification_ (Downers Grove, IL: InterVarstiy Press, 2001), 75-105; Also cf. the relevant exegesis in Thomas R. Schreiner, _The Law and Its Fulfillment_ (Grand Rapids: Baker Books, 1993); D. A. Carson, Peter T. O'Brien,

outlook of the new perspective. Although its origins can be traced back further,[13] the work of E.P. Sanders has been most influential in this movement.[14] Two other English-speaking scholars who have been considered key representatives of the movement are James Dunn and N.T. Wright. Wright, who has written masterfully on such issues as the resurrection and the historical Jesus, has probably been most influential among evangelicals because he, more than most, comes from an evangelical perspective.[15] The new perspective on Paul began with a new perspective on Second Temple Judaism (the Judaism of Paul's day). It has been argued that the Judaism of Paul's day was not a works-righteousness religion but a religion of grace. Protestants, according to these scholars, have been anachronistic by reading later Judaism into the Second

---

and Mark Seifrid, *Justification and Variegated Nomism. Volume 1: Complexities of Second Temple Judaism* (Tubingen: Mohr Siebeck; Grand Rapids: Baker Academic, 2001); Mark Seifrid, *Christ, Our Righteousness: Paul's Theology of Justification* (Downers Grove, IL: InterVarsity Press, 2000); Simon J. Gathercole, *Where is Boasting: Early Jewish Soteriology and Paul's Response in Romans 1-5* (Grand Rapids: Eerdmans, 2002); John Piper, *The Future of Justification: A Response to N.T. Wright* (Wheaton, IL: Crossway, 2007); Michael F. Bird, "When the Dust Finally Settles: Coming to a Post-New Perspective Perspective," *Criswell Theological Review* 2, no. 2 (Spring 2005).

[13] Claude Montefiore, George Foot Moore, W.D. Davies (the father-in-law of E.P. Sanders!), and Krister Stendahl are some of the scholars who are considered pre-figures of the new perspective.

[14] E.g. *Paul and Palestinian Judaism: A Comparison of Patterns of Religion* (Philadelphia: Fortress, 1977).

[15] See Rich Lusk, "N.T. Wright and Reformed Theology: Friends or Foes," *Reformation and Revival Journal* 11, no. 2 (Spring 2002): 34-53.

Temple period. Some new perspective scholars accuse Protestants of reading Paul with "Lutheran lenses," equating the Judaizers with the Roman Catholic Church. According to the new perspective, Paul was not converted because of a guilty conscience, but because he realized that Christ was Israel's messiah. As Sanders puts it, "this is what Paul finds wrong with Judaism: it is not Christianity."[16] The study of the Second Temple Period forced exegetes to go back to the text of Scripture and re-interpret Paul accordingly. According to their reading, justification no longer involves how a person gets right with God, but involves who is part of the covenant community. "Works of the law" are not about obeying the Mosaic Covenant but about ethnic boundary markers such as circumcision, food laws, and the Sabbath. Obviously, this orientation calls historic Protestantism into question. Let's paraphrase Galatians 2:16a as a test case (yet we know that a person is not justified by works of the law but through faith in Jesus Christ). Protestants have historically interpreted this to mean that sinners are not declared to be in the right by obeying the law but by believing in Jesus. The new perspective generally reads it as: a person is not included in the covenant community by following Jewish ceremonies but by believing in Jesus (or by Jesus' faithfulness). I will seek to show exegetically, that the new perspective is fundamentally wrong.[17]

---

[16] Sanders, Paul and Palestinian Judaism, 552.

[17] There have been many good insights from the new perspective on Paul. Because of their writing, evangelicals have been forced back to Scripture, which is always profitable. After all, our commitment is not to the Protestant tradition, but to the inscripurated text. Other

Imputation has historically been considered fundamental to justification in Paul, but is also under attack today as well.[18] The new perspective proponents obviously deny imputation,[19] but the doctrine is even being questioned by "evangelicals" who oppose the new perspective on Paul. Various biblical scholars are teaching that the notion of imputation is not found in Paul's writings. It is with these controversies in mind that we proceed to examine Paul's theology of justification.

Justification

Many scholars since the time of the Reformation have considered justification to be the center of Paul's theology,

---

helpful concerns raised are: an emphasis on the corporate realities of the NT (especially in our individualistic context), the necessity of obedience, the priority of exegesis, the absolute centrality of salvation-history in Paul's writings, and the importance of the unity of God's people. Generally speaking, the early Reformation tradition focused too narrowly on anthropology while the new perspective focuses too narrowly on salvation history. Both are important.

[18] Though outside the scope of this book, Federal Vision (or Auburn Avenue) theology should be mentioned. It is another movement questioning the historic understanding of justification. All of its representatives are Presbyterians who hold to a consistent Covenant Theology, with its key leaders being Douglas Wilson, James Jordan, Steve Wilkins, and Rich Lusk.

[19] N.T Wright writes, "If we use the language of law court, it makes no sense whatever to say that the judge imputes, imparts, bequeaths, conveys or otherwise transfers his righteousness to either the plaintiff or the defendant. Righteousness is not an object, a substance or a gas which can be passed across the courtroom," in *What Saint Paul Really Said* (Grand Rapids: Eerdmans, 1997), 98.

but this too has been debated.[20] Paul uses the verb "to justify (*dikaioō*)" fourteen times and "righteousness (*dikaiōsynē*)" fifty-two times with most uses occurring in Romans and Galatians. The verb "to justify" is only found outside of these two letters in 1 Corinthians 6:11 and Titus 3:7.[21] This has led some scholars to believe that Paul only formed and used the doctrine of justification for polemical reasons. Albert Schweitzer considered justification a "subsidiary crater" formed within the main crater of the mystical doctrine of redemption through being "in Christ."[22] Discovering the center of Paul's theology is beyond the scope of this book, but it must be stated that although justification *is not* the center of his theology, it is close.[23] Justification is of great importance and prominence in Paul's theology, because, as Thomas Schreiner writes, "it focuses on the basis upon which believers enter into a

---

[20] Concerning justification taking precedence, Herman Ridderbos writes, "One can ask himself, therefore, whether the traditional order of treatment which begins with the doctrine of justification is not one-sided and does not involve even the danger of a certain narrowing of viewpoint," *Paul: An Outline of his Theology* (Grand Rapids: Eerdmans, 1975), 160.

[21] George Eldon Ladd, *A Theology of the New Testament* (Grand Rapids: Eerdmans, 1974), 479.

[22] Albert Schweitzer, *The Mysticism of the Apostle Paul* (New York: Henry Holt, 1931), 225 quoted in Ladd, *A Theology of the New Testament*. For a similar perspective, see James S. Stewart, *A Man in Christ* (New York: Harper and Brothers, 1935).

[23] Quoted in Frank Thielman, *Theology of the New Testament* (Grand Rapids: Zondervan, 2005), 472. On methodology and Pauline theology, see Richard B. Gaffin Jr., *Resurrection and Redemption* (Phillipsburg, NJ: P&R Publishing, 1978), 17-30.

relationship with God."[24] Justification is one of many metaphors of salvation, but it is crucial for Paul because it provides forgiveness of sins, which is the primary need for all persons, since all persons are "in Adam." All have sinned and are under God's wrath for doing so (Rom 1:18-3:20). We are bent on evil, curved in on ourselves and God hates evildoers (Ps 5:5, 7:11) and will punish sinners for eternity, unless they repent and believe in his Son (John 3:36). One must understand sin and its consequences before understanding the death and resurrection of Jesus Christ and the justification of *the ungodly* (Rom 4:5).[25] Universal fallenness, not ethnic differences, is the urgent question the apostle Paul is seeking to answer with the doctrine of justification.[26]

Old Testament Background

Before examining the meaning of justification in Paul, it is necessary to look at the Old Testament background, which informed most aspects of Paul's theology. Righteousness in the OT can refer to God's saving activity on behalf of his people (cf. Judges 5:11, 1 Sam 12:7, Mic 6:5). The language of righteousness and salvation are often parallel in Scripture, especially in the Psalms and in

---

[24] Thomas R. Schreiner, *Paul: Apostle of God's Glory in Christ* (Downers Grove, IL: IVP Academic, 2001), 193.

[25] On this notion, see Richard B. Gaffin, Jr., "Atonement in the Pauline Corpus," in *The Glory of the Atonement*, ed. Charles E. Hill and Frank A. James III (Downers Grove, IL: InterVarsity Press, 2004), 140-62.

[26] Seifrid, *Christ, Our Righteousness*, 64. Seifrid rhetorically asks, "Did Paul need the 'word of the cross' to tell him that selfish nationalism was wrong?" Ibid., 20.

Isaiah.[27] Consider Psalm 98:2-3 which reads, "The Lord has made known his salvation; he has revealed his righteousness in the sight of the nations. He has remembered his steadfast love and faithfulness to the house of Israel. All the ends of the earth have seen the salvation of our God." Here it is clear that God's righteousness signifies an act of God in which his salvation, steadfast love, and faithfulness are displayed.[28] Isaiah 51:5-8 says, "My righteousness draws near, my salvation has gone out, and my arms will judge the peoples … but my salvation will be forever, and my righteousness will never be dismayed…but my righteousness will be forever, and my salvation to all generations."

Because of texts like these and others, it is common for scholars today to define God's righteousness as his covenant faithfulness,[29] but Mark Seifrid has shown that the words *covenant,* and *righteousness* rarely occur in the same context in the Hebrew Bible. This being the case, it would be remarkable for God's righteousness to be defined as his covenant faithfulness.[30] God's righteousness is

---

[27] Schreiner, *Paul,* 198.

[28] Seifrid, *Christ, Our Righteousness,* 39. Seifrid also points to Is 9:7, 11:4, 32:16, 33:5, 41:10, 42:21, 45:8, 21, 23, 24, 46:13, 48:18, 51:5, 6, 8, 54:14, 17, 56:1, 58:8, 59:9, 16-17, 60:17, 61:10-11, 62:1, 63:1, Ps 9:4, 22:31, 24:5, 31:1, 35:24, 36:6-7, 40:9-10, 51:14, 69:27-28, 71:15, 16, 71:19, 24, 72:1-3, 88:12, 89:15-17, 97:6, 98:2, 99:4, 103:6, 116:5, 118:19-21, 119:23, 140, 129:4, 143:1, 11, 145:7.

[29] E.g. see Sam K. Williams, "The "Righteousness of God" in Romans," *Journal of Biblical Literature* 99, no. 2 (1980): 241-90; Wright, *What Saint Paul Really Said.*

[30] See Mark A. Seifrid, "Righteousness Language in the Hebrew Scriptures and Early Judaism: Linguistic Considerations Critical to

certainly in fulfillment of his covenantal promises, but should not be *defined as* his covenantal faithfulness.[31] Some exegetes, including Seifrid, wrongly root God's righteousness in creation.[32] While it is true theologically, and a case can be made from some OT texts that God's righteousness is his faithfulness to all creation, this view lacks a strong exegetical basis from Paul's letters.[33] Ernst Kasemann is a very significant and influential interpreter of Paul, especially concerning God's righteousness. He sees in this phrase a very multi-faceted concept consisting of gift, power, and faithfulness to the creation. For Paul, he writes, the righteousness of God is "God's sovereignty over the world revealing itself eschatologically in Jesus."[34] One can see how God's righteousness is central to Kasemann's system, but he is reading far more into Paul than the text will allow. Similarly, Scott Hafemann writes, "God's righteousness consists, therefore, in his unswerving

---

the Interpretation of Paul", in D.A. Carson (ed.), *Justification and Variegated Nomism, Volume 1: The Complexities of Second Temple Judaism* (Tubingen and Grand Rapids, MI: Mohr Siebeck, 2001); Seifrid, *Christ, Our Righteousness,* 39-40; Westerholm, *Perspectives,* 286ff.

[31] Westerholm, *Perspectives,* 292; Thomas R. Schreiner, *Romans,* Baker Exegetical Commentary on the New Testament (Grand Rapids: Baker Academic, 1998), 69. Also see Schreiner, *Paul,* 199.

[32] Seifrid, Christ, Our Righteousness, 40-45.

[33] Douglas Moo writes, "Paul's righteousness language appears to be concentrated solely on the relationship of God to people," The Epistle to the Romans, New International Commentary on the New Testament (Grand Rapids: Eerdmans, 1996), 89; Schreiner, Paul, 197.

[34] Ernst Kasemann, New Testament Questions for Today (Philadelphia: Fortress Press, 1969), 180.

commitment to glorify himself by maintaining his moral standards in judgment, by revealing his sovereignty in election, and by showing his loving mercy through meeting the needs of his people."[35] One wonders what is *not included* in the concept of God's righteousness.[36] Again, these are true *theologically* (i.e. true from other texts), but these themes cannot be sustained from honest exegesis of the Pauline letters.

John Piper has argued that God's righteousness is "his unswerving commitment to preserve and display the glory of his name."[37] This is also certainly true theologically, but exegetically questionable. It is more accurate to say that God's righteousness, along with every other activity of God, is *rooted in* his commitment and desire to glorify himself above all else. God's righteousness in the Old Testament is often understood in a forensic (legal) context. In Deuteronomy 25:1, Israel's judges were commanded to "acquit [or justify] the innocent and condemn the guilty."

[35] Scott J. Hafemann, The NIV Application Commentary: Second Corinthians (Grand Rapids: Zondervan, 2000), 369.

[36] Michael Bird goes so far as to say, "Thus the righteousness of God, at least in Rom 1.17, introduces the entire package of salvation including justification, redemption, propitiatory sacrifice, forgiveness of sins, membership in the new covenant community, reconciliation, the gift of the Holy Spirit, power for a new obedience, union with Christ, freedom from sin, and eschatological vindication. God's righteousness is an all-encompassing action that includes both redemption and renewal," *The Saving Righteousness of God* (Eugene, OR: Wipf & Stock Publishers, 2007), 16.

[37] John Piper, *The Justification of God: An Exegetical and Theological Study of Romans 9:1-23* (Grand Rapids: Baker Books, 1993), 103. Also see Piper, *The Future of Justification*, 62ff.

Clearly, to condemn is to *declare* to be wicked, not to make the person wicked, just as justifying the innocent is to *declare* righteous not to make righteous. Job "justifies" himself rather than God. The just God "will not acquit the wicked" (Exodus 23:7).[38] Paul also uses righteousness language in a forensic context.

Justification in Paul

Justification in Paul refers to God's verdict of not-guilty at the final judgment, brought into the present by faith.[39] The verb "to justify" (*dikaioō*) is built off of the same root as "righteous" (*dikaios*) and "righteousness" (*dikaiosynē*). Ladd summarizes justification as follows: "The root idea in justification is the declaration of God, the righteous judge, that those who believe in Christ, sinful though they may be, are righteous—are viewed as being righteous, because in Christ they have come into a righteous relationship with God."[40] The meaning of "righteousness of God" in Paul is fiercely debated as well,[41] but it is almost universally agreed that the verb "to justify" is strictly forensic, that is, it is a declaration.[42] Romans 8:33 says, "Who shall bring any charge against God's elect? It is God who justifies." Romans 2:13b says, "the doers of the law will be justified," that is, vindicated in the divine law court on the last day.

---

[38] D.A Carson, "Reflections on Salvation and Justification in the New Testament," *Journal of the Evangelical Theological Society* 40, no. 4 (December 1997): 589.

[39] Thomas R. Schreiner, *New Testament Theology: Magnifying God in Christ* (Grand Rapids: Baker, forthcoming), 271-72.

[40] Ladd, *A Theology of the New Testament*, 478.

[41] See Bird, *The Saving Righteousness of God*, 6-39.

[42] Ladd, *A Theology of the New Testament*, 484.

Several texts contrast being justified by faith and by works of the law (Gal 2:16-17, 3:11, 24, 5:4, Rom 3:20-30, 5:1). No one is justified by works of the law. God justifies the *ungodly* (Rom 4:5). Justification by faith is contrasted with justification by works, showing that the one who has faith in Christ is *declared* to be in the right before God.[43]

We have seen that the OT conception of God's righteousness is forensic. Though Paul uses the "righteous" word group in a number of ways, "righteousness of God" is fundamentally forensic when used in contexts explaining the work of God in Christ (Rom 1:17, 3:21-22, 10:3, 2 Cor 5:21, Phil 3:9).[44] Scholars usually opt for one of three views on "the righteousness of God": 1) An attribute of God, 2) A status given by God, or 3) An activity of God.[45] In the present author's opinion, Moo's exegesis is closest to Paul when he defines "righteousness of God" as an activity of God by which he brings people into a right relationship with himself. This activity of making right is purely forensic, but as we will see, God does not stop with a mere declaration. God gives us his Spirit and empowers us to live transformed lives. That is just not what the Bible means when it uses the language of justification. Using law court imagery, it is an activity of the judge that is a declaration of status, "an act that results in, and indeed includes within it, a gift.[46] Many scholars see the phrase as both

---

[43] Schreiner, *Paul*, 204.

[44] Thielman, *Theology of the New Testament*, 346

[45] Moo, *Romans*, 70-71.

[46] Ibid., 74-75. Westerholm writes, "If the term does not refer to his own gift of (extraordinary) righteousness to sinners (cf. Phil. 3:9; also Rom. 5:17; 10:3), it speaks of the salvific act by which God declares

transformative and forensic.[47] Some (Kasemann & followers) have sought to distinguish "righteousness of God" as a technical term for Paul, but the evidence for this claim is simply lacking,[48] plus Paul uses the phrase in strikingly similar ways.[49] Philippians 3:8b-9 is crucial here, where Paul writes, "in order that I may gain Christ and be found in him, not having a righteousness of my own that comes from the law, but that which comes through faith in Christ, the righteousness *from* God (*tēn ek theou dikaiosynēn*) that depends on faith." Concerning this verse, Tom Schreiner writes, "The contrast between 'the righteousness from God' and 'my own righteousness' in this verse— Paul's contrast between his devotion to the law and his newfound allegiance to Christ—indicates that 'the righteousness from God' here is a divine gift."[50] Paul's use of righteousness in Philippians 3:9 is undoubtedly forensic. The righteousness of God is a gift.

---

sinners righteous," *Perspectives*, 390. Similarly, Cornelis Venema writes, "Against the background of the Old Testament idea of God's righteousness, the apostle Paul is affirming that the gospel of Jesus Christ reveals God's judicial action in securing the righteous status of his people before him," *Getting the Gospel Right*, (Carlisle, PA: The Banner of Truth Trust, 2006), 73.

[47] See Schreiner, *Romans*, 63-71. Schreiner has since corrected his view: Compare *Paul*, 203-09 and *New Testament Theology*, 274-80 where he argues for a forensic view and against the transformative view.

[48] See Moo, *Romans*, 81-86.

[49] In the following two paragraphs, I am indebted to the exegetical insight in Schreiner, *Paul*, 200f; Westerholm, *Perspectives*, 284-85, 390.

[50] Ibid.

Williams and others object that "righteousness from God" is not identical to "righteousness of God." We appreciate the precision in which Williams tries to handle the text, but he is guilty of reading Paul in too technical a manner.[51] This is confirmed by noting the contexts of the texts involved. Both Romans 1:17 and 3:21-22 are centered on one's relationship to God. Does a person relate to God by faith, or through the law? Romans 10:3 is strikingly similar to Philippians 3:9, where Paul writes, "For, being ignorant of the righteousness that comes from God, and seeking to establish their own, they did not submit to God's righteousness." Both Paul and Israel of old were seeking to secure their own righteousness instead of receiving the gift of righteousness given to those who place their faith in Christ.[52] Paul sets up the universal dilemma in Romans 1:18-3:20, concluding with the words, "For by works of the law no human being will be justified in his sight" (3:20a). The next verses give the solution: "But now the righteousness of God has been manifested apart from law...the righteousness of God through faith in Jesus Christ for all who believe" (3:21-22). To summarize and paraphrase: No person can secure their own righteousness by obedience to the law's demands, but now the

---

[51] Williams, "Righteousness of God" in Romans, 258-59.

[52] Schreiner lists 4 parallels in Rom. 10:1-5 and Phil. 3:2-9: 1) a reference to God's righteousness 2) the contrast between righteousness by law and righteousness by faith 3) the parallel between Israel's quest to establish its own righteousness and Paul's quest to do the same 4) Paul's emphasis on "not having a righteousness of my own that comes from the law" (Phil 3:9), and Israel's attempt to establish its own righteousness (Rom 10:3)—a "righteousness that is based on the law" (10:5), *New Testament Theology*, 276.

eschatological vindicating activity of God has been revealed apart from the law covenant for all who believe in Christ.[53]

Second Corinthians 5:21 is also an extremely important text in this debate. In it, we read, "For our sake he made him to be sin who knew no sin, so that in him we might become the righteousness of God."[54] The forensic idea of God's righteousness is clearly present in this verse.[55] God made Christ sin (legally) so that in him we might become the righteousness of God (legally).[56] The heart of becoming the righteousness of God includes forgiveness of sins (cf. 2 Cor 5:19). Brian Vickers writes, "For Paul then to speak of "becoming the righteousness of God" indicates that the barrier between God and man, namely sin, has been removed, but this does not involve a transformation (though transformation certainly follows)—it involves a legal decision based on just grounds."[57] The substitutionary sacrifice of Christ is clearly present; Christ was reckoned sin so that we could be reckoned righteous in him. So, God's righteousness cannot be limited only to his saving

---

[53] For more on these verses, see D. A. Carson, "Atonement in Romans 3:21-26," in *The Glory of the Atonement*, ed. Charles E. Hill and Frank A. James III (Downers Grove, IL: InterVarsity Press, 2004), 119-39.

[54] For a penetrating analysis and defense of the forensic understanding of this verse, see Brian Vickers, *Jesus' Blood and Righteousness* (Wheaton, IL: Crossway, 2006), 159-190.

[55] Wright's exegetical conclusion on this verse teaching that becoming the righteousness of God is "an incarnation of the covenant faithfulness of God" is just plain silly, *What Saint Paul Really Said*, 104-05.

[56] Ridderbos, *Paul*, 168.

[57] Vickers, *Jesus' Blood*, 172.

righteousness. In the cross of Christ, both the saving and judging righteousness of God meet. Wrath and mercy kiss at the cross. God judges and condemns his Son so that he can justify the ungodly and not compromise his justice (Rom 3:25-26).[58] The justification of God and the justification of the one who trusts Christ are bound together.[59]

Some scholars teach that justification is not so much about how one gets right with God (soteriology), but about how one becomes a member of the covenant community (ecclesiology).[60] Recently, Michael Bird has proposed a *via media* (middle way) between the traditional view and the insights from the new perspective, arguing that justification must be viewed as both forensic declaration *and* covenant membership.[61] This is an attractive view, for traditional Reformed theology has at times neglected the corporate and communal aspects of Paul's theology, but this view is finally unconvincing. Covenant membership is obviously absolutely vital for the apostle Paul (cf. Gal 2:11-14), but the text will not allow covenant membership to be pushed under the umbrella of "righteousness" language. Covenant membership is a fundamental *implication*, or

---

[58] Seifrid writes, "When God works salvation for his people, he establishes justice for them (and for himself) over against their enemies and his. Saving righteousness and wrath parallel one another, since they are different aspects of the same event," *Christ, Our Righteousness*, 43.

[59] Ibid., 66.

[60] See Wright, *What Saint Paul Really Said* for a key representative of this viewpoint.

[61] Bird, *The Saving Righteousness of God*, 113-54.

result of justification.[62] We do not gain a right relationship with God by being counted among his covenant community, but rather we become part of the covenant community by virtue of the right standing we are given in Christ.[63]

Other scholars accuse the view proposed in this book of being a "legal fiction." However, this objection holds no weight though because the gift of righteousness is *real*. God's wrath *has been removed* and there is now no condemnation for the believer in Christ.[64] Ladd writes, "One's relationship to God is no fiction."[65] This forensic declaration is just as real as one's life in the Spirit. Justification is *one* aspect of the multi-faceted salvation found in union with Christ. Every aspect of salvation cannot be subsumed under "righteousness" in Paul.

---

[62] Richard B. Gaffin Jr. writes, "For Paul, justification undoubtedly had inalienable ecclesiological implications and these are a prominent concern, especially in Galatians. These implications must not be denied, obscured or downplayed through an unduly individualistic soteriological mindset. No doubt, too, they have not been appreciated heretofore as they should. But justification in Paul is essentially, primarily soteriological. It is a 'transfer' term describing what takes place in an individual's transition from wrath to grace, a component of what is effected at the point of being 'delivered from the domain of darkness and transferred into the kingdom of his beloved Son' (Col 1:13)," *By Faith, Not By Sight: Paul and the Order of Salvation* (Waynesboro, GA: Paternoster Press, 2006), 45.

[63] Paul A. Rainbow, *The Way of Salvation: The Role of Christian Obedience in Justifications* (Waynesboro, GA: Paternoster Press, 2005), 104 n. 22.

[64] See Vickers, *Jesus' Blood*, 216-22, where he carefully lays this objection to rest.

[65] Ladd, *A Theology of the New Testament*, 486.

The Ground of Justification and Imputation

The ground of justification is the death and resurrection of Jesus Christ. Romans 5:9 says, "we have been justified by his blood."[66] The ground of justification is not to be found in our works, our faith, or the Spirit's work in us, but in the objective work of the risen Christ.[67] "If justification were through the law, then Christ died for no purpose" (Gal 2:21). Romans 3:21-26 is a crucial passage on salvation in Christ in the letter to Romans and indeed in the whole New Testament.[68] The previous section can be summarized by 3:10 and 3:23: None is righteous, no not one, for all have sinned and fallen short of the glory of God.[69] Paul gives us the solution to the problem of universal fallenness in 3:21-26, as D.A. Carson rightly notes: "The problem is not first and foremost the failure of Israel (national or otherwise), or inappropriate use of the law, or the urgency of linking Jews and Gentiles (all genuine themes in these chapters), but the wrath of God directed against every human being, Jew and Gentile alike—a wrath elicited by universal human wickedness."[70] All are condemned, "but now" in this new epoch of redemptive history inaugurated by Christ, the

---

[66] See Leon Morris, *The Apostolic Preaching of the Cross* (Grand Rapids: Eerdmans, 1965), 112-28, who has shown the "blood" in Scripture means "death by violence."

[67] Ladd, *A Theology of the New Testament,* 489.

[68] C.E.B. Cranfield goes as far as to say that this short section is the center and heart of the whole letter in *A Critical and Exegetical Commentary on the Epistle to the Romans,* The International Critical Commentary (Edinburgh: T & T Clark, 1975), 1:199.

[69] Ibid., 104.

[70] Carson, "Atonement in Romans 3:21-26," 120.

eschatological justifying activity of God is available for all who believe. Believers "are justified by his grace as a gift, through the redemption that is in Christ Jesus" (3:24). Christ was set forth to absorb the wrath of God on behalf of those who believe.[71] God did this to demonstrate that he takes sin seriously, and does not simply sweep it under the rug. Without the cross of Christ, God's justice could be called into question, but God takes his name extremely seriously so he pours out his wrath on his Son to demonstrate that he is just and yet the justifier of the ungodly (3:26).[72]

As stated above, many scholars are denying imputation as a legitimate Pauline teaching. Significantly, imputation is being questioned both by scholars who adhere to *and* deny the new perspective.[73] Historically, imputation has been viewed as a near corollary to justification in Paul. What are we to make of this debate? It must be frankly admitted, with George Ladd, that "Paul never expressly states that the righteousness of Christ is imputed to

---

[71] See Morris, *Apostolic Preaching,* 144-213.

[72] In verse 25, righteousness takes on a different meaning (also cf. 3:5, 9:14). Here Piper's definition is fitting: "His absolute faithfulness always to act for his name's sake and for the preservation and display of his glory," *Justification of God,* 150. Moo opts for "God's 'consistency' in always acting in accordance with his own character," *The Epistle to the Romans,* 240.

[73] Robert Gundry is one of the major evangelical advocates against imputation. See John Piper, *Counted Righteous in Christ* (Wheaton, IL: Crossway Books, 2002) for a response primarily aimed at Gundry.

believers."[74] Should we conclude that imputation is not in the text but simply a systematic category imposed on Paul? No, the solution is found in Paul's "in Christ" language. Herman Ridderbos writes, "The foundation for the doctrine of justification, too, lies in the corporate unity of Christ and his own."[75] Imputation takes place in union with the risen Christ.[76] Indeed, being incorporated into Christ, who is righteous, is the grounding for imputation.[77] Calvin sums this viewpoint up nicely:

> Christ, having been made ours, makes us sharers with him in the gifts with which he has been endowed. We do not, therefore, contemplate him outside ourselves from afar in order that his righteousness may be imputed to us but because we put on Christ and are engrafted into his body — in

---

[74] Ladd, *A Theology of the New Testament*, 491. So also Morris, who writes, "he never says in so many words that the righteousness of Christ was imputed to believers," in *Apostolic Preaching*, 282; Seifrid also says, "It is worth observing that Paul never speaks of Christ's righteousness as imputed to believers, as became standard in Protestantism," in *Christ, Our Righteousness*, 174.

[75] Ridderbos, *Paul*, 169.

[76] For very fine treatments of union with Christ, see Gaffin, *By Faith, Not by Sight*; John Murray, *Redemption Accomplished and Applied* (Grand Rapids: Eerdmans, 1955), 161-73; Michael S. Horton, *Covenant and Salvation* (Westminster John Knox Press: Louisville, KY, 2007); Robert Letham, *The Work of Christ* (Downers Grove, IL: InterVarsity Press, 1993), 75-87; Anthony A. Hoekema, *Saved By Grace* (Grand Rapids, MI: Eerdmans, 1989), 54-67.

[77] D. A. Carson, "The Vindication of Imputation," in *Justification in Perspective*, ed. Bruce L. McCormack (Grand Rapids, MI: Baker Academic, 2006), 72.

short, because he deigns to make us one with him. For this reason, we glory that we have fellowship with him.[78]

Paul writes "He is the source of your life in Christ Jesus, whom God made our wisdom and our righteousness and sanctification and redemption" (1 Cor 1:30). It is "in him" that we become the righteousness of God (2 Cor 5:21, also cf. Gal 2:11-21, Gal 3:13-14, Rom 5:18-19). Galatians 2:17 says, "In our endeavor to be justified *in Christ* (my italics), and Romans 8:1 says, "There is therefore now no condemnation for those who are *in Christ Jesus*" (my italics). In Philippians 3:7-9, Paul wants to count his former gain as loss, in order to gain Christ, "and be found *in him*, not having a righteousness of my own that comes from the law, but that which comes through faith in Christ, the righteousness from God that depends on faith" (my italics).

By faith, Christ becomes the covenantal head of the believer. Once in Adam (Eph 2:1-3, Rom 5:12-21), the believer is now in Christ through faith. Adam's sin brought condemnation (clearly legal), while Christ's act of obedience brings justification and life (Rom 5:18). Christ is the representative head, acting on behalf of his people. "For as in Adam all die, so also in Christ shall all be made alive" (1 Cor 15:22). His death ensures forgiveness of sins and his resurrection brings about our justification (Rom 4:25).[79] His resurrection is *his* justification and we share in his

---

[78] John Calvin, *Institutes of the Christian Religion* 3.11.10, 737. For more on Calvin's views on union with Christ and justification, see Crag B. Carpenter, "A Question of Union with Christ? Calvin and Trent on Justification," *Westminster Theological Journal* 64, no. 2 (2002): 363-86.

[79] Seifrid, Christ, Our Righteousness, 46-47.

justification through faith-union with him (1 Tim 3:16).[80]
For this reason and more, Michael Bird offers the proposal
to drop the language of imputed righteousness and speak
instead of "incorporated righteousness."[81] He argues that
"incorporated righteousness" is what takes place at the
exegetical level, but maintains that imputation is an
appropriate label within the discourse of *systematic theology*.
The present author thinks imputation should be kept,
because after all, the word is derived from Scripture:
Abraham believed God and it was *counted* to him as
righteousness (Rom 4:3). Carson shows the parallel in
Romans 4 as follows:

> 4:5 God justifies the ungodly

---

[80] Gaffin, Resurrection, 119-24; By Faith, Not By Sight, 84-85. Herman
Ridderbos writes, "Because the church is in Christ, His resurrection
is her justification," When the Time Had Fully Come (Scarsdale,
NY: Westminster Publishing House, 1982), 56. Lane G. Tipton
writes, "Jesus' resurrection is an eschatological demonstration and
judicial declaration that the Son of God has been vindicated as
righteous," "Union with Christ and Justification," in Justification in
Christ, ed. by K. Scott Oliphint (Great Britain: Mentor, 2007), 30. For
more on the importance of Christ's resurrection and justification,
see Bird, The Saving Righteousness of God, 40-59, where he writes,
"Consequently, union with Christ is union with the justified
Messiah and the now Righteous One. Jesus by fact of his
resurrection is the locus of righteousness and redemption (cf. 1 Cor
1.30; 2 Cor 5.21; Eph 1.17) and believers are justified only because
they have been united with the justified Messiah. Whereas believers
formerly shared the verdict of condemnation pronounced on Adam,
now they partake of the verdict of justification pronounced on
Christ," 56.

[81] Bird, *The Saving Righteousness of God*, 40-87.

4:6 God credits righteousness apart from works[82]

Carson, with Bird, also shows that the different domains of discourse (exegesis and theology) must be kept in mind. Strictly speaking, no passage in Paul says that our sins are imputed to Christ and his righteousness to us, but considering Paul's "in Christ" language and the synthesis of several key texts, we can say that imputation is "an unavoidable logical conclusion."[83]

Those scholars who want to subsume transformation under Paul's "righteousness" language also neglect Paul's doctrine of being "in Christ,"[84] which is more comprehensive than the categories tied to righteousness/justification language.[85] Paul's "in Christ"

---

[82] Carson, "The Vindication of Imputation," 61.

[83] Ladd, *A Theology of the New Testament*, 491; Brian Vickers has recently written an important defense of imputation. He focuses on Romans 4, 5:19, and 2 Corinthians 5:21. His conclusions are similar to Carson, and Bird's. He writes, "It is difficult to overemphasize that the imputation of Christ's righteousness takes place in union with Christ. Only as a person is identified with Christ is Christ's righteousness imputed to that person. Another way of saying this is that Christ's righteousness is counted to the believer because God now sees the believer only in relation to Christ and his accomplished work," Vickers, *Jesus' Blood*, 237.

[84] For example, Peter Stuhlmacher writes, "Therefore, the controversial and [sic]—between Protestants and Catholics since the sixteenth century—much discussed distinction between 'imputed' righteousness (which is only credited to the sinner) and 'effective' righteousness (which transforms the sinner in his or her being) cannot be maintained from the Pauline texts," *Revisiting Paul's Doctrine of Justification* (Downers Grove, IL: InterVarsity Press, 2001), 62.

[85] Carson, "The Vindication of Imputation," 76.

language (union with Christ) allows him to speak in
transformative and legal categories simultaneously without
conflating either into the other (1 Cor 1:30, 6:11).[86] Forensic
and transformative elements do not stand over against one
another for Paul, but both are to be found in union with the
risen Christ.[87] Being declared righteous (justification) and
life in the Spirit (sanctification) are both distinguishable but
inseparable facets of being united to Christ by faith. Adam's
fall has left the world guilty *and* enslaved and Christ and
the Spirit overcome both.[88] So in justification, the believer
has a right standing with God, but this status is
accompanied with the power of the Spirit.[89] Paul could not
imagine a person who has been justified yet continues to
live in the flesh (Rom 6:7). Union with Christ (itself a
forensic reality) is the *objective* basis for God's transforming
work through the Spirit. To speak of changed lives without
God's declaration of righteous, or God's declaration of
righteous without changed lives is to do a great injustice to
Paul's theology.[90]

The Instrument of Justification

The ground of justification is the death and resurrection
of Christ, but the instrument of justification is faith. Ladd
helpfully defines faith as "acceptance of this work of God

---

[86] Tipton, "Union with Christ and Justification," 38.

[87] Ridderbos writes, "For being in Christ implies both, the forensic as
well as the pneumatic," *When the Time Had Fully Come,* 56. Calvin,
Institutes, 3.16.1, 798.

[88] Gaffin, *By Faith, Not By Sight,* 33-35.

[89] Vickers, *Jesus' Blood,* 174. Also see Carson, "Reflections on Salvation,"
602.

[90] Schreiner, *Paul,* 207-08.

in Christ, complete reliance upon it, and an utter abandonment of one's works as the grounds of justification."[91] In Galatians 2:16, Paul insists three different times that "a person is not justified by works of the law but through faith in Jesus Christ" (also cf. Rom 3:28). "Works of the law" in Paul should be taken as "actions demanded by the Mosaic law."[92] In Paul's gospel, the righteousness of God is revealed through faith from first to last (Rom 1:17 TNIV). God's righteousness has been revealed "through faith in Jesus Christ for all who believe" (Rom 3:22).[93] Faith is the exclusive means for salvation in Christ. It is not faith in and of itself that saves however; Rather Christ saves through faith. Neither is it a mere "faith in faith," but saving faith is always a Christ-centered faith. This is important to stress in our day where a vague notion of faith is gaining popularity. Biblical faith has a definite content to it.

Concerning faith and obedience the Reformation motto has rightly been that we are justified by faith alone, but

---

[91] Ladd, *A Theology of the New Testament*, 490.

[92] For this interpretation, see Schreiner, *The Law and Its Fulfillment*, 44-71; idem, *New Testament Theology*, 526-28; Douglas J. Moo, "'Law,' 'Works of the Law,' and Legalism in Paul," *Westminster Theological Journal* 45, no. 1 (Spring 1983): 90-99; Douglas Moo, *The Epistle to the Romans*, 211-17; Schreiner, *Romans*, 168-74; Westerholm, *Perspectives*, 313-21, 367 n45, 371 n 55.

[93] Many scholars today argue that "faith in Jesus Christ" should be rendered "the faith/faithfulness of Jesus Christ. For arguments for the traditional rendering, see Carson, "Atonement in Romans 3:21-26," 125-27; Schreiner, *Romans*, 181-86; idem, *Paul*, 211-216; idem, *New Testament Theology*, 574ff; Westerholm, *Perspectives*, 305 n18.

faith is never alone.[94] Faith and obedience are distinct but absolutely inseparable (see James 2:14-26). Paul introduces and closes the book of Romans writing that he is seeking to bring about the obedience which flows from faith among all the nations (Rom 1:5, 16:26). In the new creation, which has been inaugurated by Christ's resurrection, faith works through love (Gal 5:6, 6:15). Paul also speaks of the work of faith (1 Thess 1:3, 2 Thess 1:11). Faith *always* goes public in acts of obedience. In Martin Luther's words, "Oh, it is a living, busy, active, mighty thing, this faith; and so it is impossible for it not to do good works incessantly. It does not ask whether there are good works to do, but before the question arises; it has already done them, and is always at the doing of them. He who does not these works is a faithless man."[95] A mere assent that does not express itself in works is false faith.[96] Tom Schreiner writes, "Faith inevitably manifests itself in obedience, so that faith is the

---

[94] Provocatively, Seifrid writes, "Justification is by works alone, but the works that justify are never alone. They are an outworking of faith, which is present with them," *Christ, Our Righteousness*, 181. See also John Calvin, *Commentaries on the Epistles of Paul to the Galatians and Ephesians*, trans. William Pringle (Grand Rapids, MI: Baker Books, 2005), 152.

[95] Martin Luther, *Commentary on Romans* (Grand Rapids: Kregel Publications, 1954), xvii.

[96] Ridderbos, *Paul*, 179-80. Similarly, Seifrid writes, "Faith which properly deserves the name has works. Mere assent is not faith, but unbelief hiding under a pseudonym," *Christ, Our Righteousness*, 180. Also see Bird, *The Saving Righteousness of God*, 172-78

seed and works are the fruit."[97] Faith is the root, and obedience is the necessary fruit.

Final Judgment

The Pauline doctrine of justification is "decidedly located in the final judgment" and "is distorted to the extent that this end-time perspective is faded out."[98] Along with many other themes and doctrines in the New Testament, justification has an already/not yet aspect. We have seen that Paul considers justification as a past event occurring when a person trusts Christ, but he can also speak of justification as future (cf. Rom 5:19, Gal 5:5, 2 Tim 4:8, Rom 2:13).[99] Believers have been justified and so *shall be saved* from the wrath of God (Rom 5:9). By faith in Jesus Christ, the final judgment for the believer *has been brought into the present*. For the believer, the final judgment has *already been executed* in the death and resurrection of Jesus Christ and is received by faith here and now.[100] The verdict of the last day has been declared in advance for those who

---

[97] Thomas R. Schreiner, "The Commands of God," in *Central Themes in Biblical Theology* ed. by Scott J. Hafemann and Paul R. House (Grand Rapids: Baker Academic, 2007), 71.

[98] Stuhlmacher, *Revisiting Paul's Doctrine of Justification*, 14, 42. On the eschatological nature of justification, see Ladd, *A Theology of the New Testament*, 482-84; Ridderbos, *Paul*, 161-66; Gaffin, *By Faith, Not By Sight*, 79-108.

[99] Romans 2 is fiercely debated. See Schreiner, The Law and Its Fulfillment, 179-204; Bird, The Saving Righteousness of God, 155-72; Piper, The Future of Justification, 105-110.

[100] Seifrid writes, "Paul regards our present justification as an accomplished reality, a real and full vindication, not as a gradual transformation which has begun within us," Christ, Our Righteousness, 148.

believe in Jesus. Paul's teaching that one is justified by faith now (Rom 5:1) and yet judged according to works (2 Cor 5:10, Rom 14:10-12, 2 Tim 4:1, 1 Cor 4:5) is not a contradiction.[101] Judgment according to works will not be a weighing of deeds, but a manifestation of persons by their works.[102] As mentioned above, Paul had no category for a person who is justified, yet does not persevere. Saving faith inevitably manifests itself in changed lives. Being united to Christ has forensic and transformative realities flowing from it. Good works are necessary for salvation, not in the sense of gaining God's favor, but as *evidence* of a salvation already given in Christ.[103] The final ground for acquittal in the final judgment is the death and resurrection of Christ, appropriated by believers through faith. There is therefore now no condemnation for those who are in Christ Jesus (Rom 8:1).

So we have seen that justification is the starting point. It is the great indicative. It is the basis of our good deeds and changed life. Obedience is called for, but it all flows from

---

[101] See Ridderbos, Paul, 178-81.

[102] Seifrid, Christ, Our Righteousness, 101. Gaffin helpfully writes, "For Christians, future judgment according to works does not operate according to a different principle than their already having been justified by faith. The difference is that the final judgment will be the open manifestation of that present justification, their being 'openly acquitted' as we have seen. And in that future judgment their obedience, their works, are not the ground or basis. Nor are they (co-) instrumental, a coordinate instrument for appropriating divine approbation as they supplement faith. Rather, they are the essential and manifest criterion of that faith," By Faith, Not By Sight, 98.

[103] Schreiner, *The Law and Its Fulfillment*, 200-204.

our right standing with God. We work *from* our justification, not *towards* it.[104] In other words, the indicative precedes the imperative.

---

[104] Horton, *The Gospel-Driven Life*, 149.

CHAPTER 2

INDICATIVE/IMPERATIVE: GOSPEL LOGIC

The Jewish people viewed resurrection in terms of a large scale event that would not occur until the end of history when their covenant God would restore the world and raise humanity to life, some to eternal life and others to eternal destruction. What they did not expect was that one man would be raised in the middle of history, as the first-fruits. Christ's resurrection was the first day of the new creation. Now, new covenant Christians live during the overlap of the ages, between the two comings of Christ. The age to come has broken into the present with the resurrection of Jesus and the giving of the Spirit. Oscar Cullman has helpfully compared the Christian life with living between D-Day and VE-Day during World War II. The allies invaded Normandy on June 6, 1944. It was called D-day and it was the decisive battle of the war. The beachhead was established and everyone knew the allies were the victors. But the final overthrow of the Nazi regime wouldn't occur until May 8, 1945. After D-day, there was never any question as to how the war would end, but there was still lots of fighting to be done. There was no way Hitler would give in. VE-Day was guaranteed, but there would still be fighting, suffering, death, and agony. In fact, more people would die after D-Day than before, but the outcome was never in doubt. This is where we live as new covenant Christians. The victory has occurred at the cross and resurrection of Israel's Messiah. Christ has guaranteed our forgiveness of sins (justification) and God's new world, but we still have to wage war and fight sin in this present world order. The second coming of Christ will be VE-Day, but it is not here yet. We live in between the times, between the already and not yet, in between God's victory, and the ultimate fulfillment of God's promises.

This leaves an undeniable tension for those who have been justified by faith in Christ and given the gift of the Spirit, yet still have indwelling sin and live in this present evil age. Our obedience to the law of Christ is always imperfect. The solution is to be found in the distinction between the gospel and its fruit, or what New Testament scholars, using grammatical terminology, have called the "Indicative and Imperative."[105] *Indicative,* meaning the fact of what God has done for his people in Christ, and *imperative* meaning what God now commands and expects from his people. Michael Horton writes, "An indicative tells us what is in fact the case: for example *the cat is on the mat.* An imperative tells us to do something: *put the cat on the mat.*"[106] It is vital to the Christian life to keep these in balance. The imperative always flows out of the indicative. The indicative always expresses itself in the imperative.

If one over-emphasizes the need for obedience and neglects the good news of what God has done for us in Christ (namely Justification, the divine declaration), there is

[105] See Thomas R. Schreiner and Ardel B. Caneday, *The Race Set Before Us* (Downers Grove, IL: InterVarsity Press, 2001), 168.
[106] Horton, *Christless Christianity,* 107.

a tendency towards legalism. Legalism never leads to true spiritual life. One of two errors usually occurs: a person will think they are doing well and end up becoming proud, and arrogant. Then when something bad happens to them, they are angry at God, because they think they deserve better. They've kept their end of the deal, so they think. The other error is to realize that you can never do enough good works to please God. We will always fail. This leads to self-hate and despair. On the other hand, if one over-emphasizes the good news of what has taken place in Christ, and does not call people to obedience, they will become worldly, and immoral, not taking God's commands seriously enough.

This relationship is really what sets Christianity over against all other religions. Pastor Tim Keller writes, "Religion operates on the principle 'I obey—therefore I am accepted by God.' But the operating principle of the gospel is 'I am accepted by God through what Christ has done—therefore I obey."[107] This is another way of saying what the Reformation tradition has said from the start: justification is the basis for sanctification. The objective work of Christ is the foundation for the subjective work of the Holy Spirit.

I hope it is clear that both the indicative and the imperative are essential. We need to be a people who understand the glorious good news of what God has done for us and in us through Christ, and be a people who are marked by obedience. Thankfully, we are not left to ourselves to find this balance. God, in his kindness, has revealed himself and

---

[107] Tim Keller, *The Reason for God* (NY: Dutton, 2008), 179-80.

continually shows us these twin truths. Here are several examples mostly found in Paul's letters:

First, it's important to note that the letters of Paul are often structured in this manner, though the distinction is not air-tight and there is often overlap.[108] Think of Ephesians: in the first three chapters we read about election, redemption, forgiveness, the gift of the Sprit, being brought to life from the dead, being brought near to Christ though we were far off, the mystery of the gospel. Then Paul turns to the imperatives of unity in the church, putting on the new self, abstaining from sexual immorality, marital relations, child-parent relations, slave-master relations, and then putting on the full armor of God. Galatians is the same way. Paul lays out four chapters of biblical theology before addressing the chief issue of circumcision. He tackles apostolic authority, justification by faith, the law in God's plan, then the first imperative comes in 4:12 and circumcision is not even mentioned until 5:2! Or consider that blessed letter to the Romans. After eleven chapters of gospel theology, Paul writes, "I appeal to you *therefore*, brothers, by the mercies of God, to present your bodies as a living sacrifice, holy and acceptable to God, which is your spiritual worship. Do not be conformed to this world, but be transformed by the renewal of your mind, that by testing you may discern what is the will of God, what is good and acceptable and perfect," (Rom 12:1-2 my italics) and then continues with a few chapters of ethical exhortation. Paul grounds the imperatives of chapters 12-16 with the indicatives of chapters 1-11.

---

[108] Horton, Christless Christianity, 156.

Romans 6:1-12 is telling in this regard. In essence he says, you have died to sin (indicative), therefore put sin to death (imperative). Read verses 1-2 coupled with verses 11-12: "What shall we say then? Are we to continue in sin that grace may abound? By no means! How can we who died to sin still live in it? ... So you also must consider yourselves dead to sin and alive to God in Christ Jesus. Let not sin therefore reign in your mortal bodies, to make you obey their passions."[109]

In Colossians 3:1-10, Paul writes, "If then you have been raised with Christ, seek the things that are above, where Christ is, seated at the right hand of God. Set your minds on things that are above, not on things that are on earth. For you have died, and your life is hidden with Christ in God. When Christ who is your life appears, then you also will appear with him in glory. Put to death therefore what is earthly in you: sexual immorality, impurity, passion, evil desire, and covetousness, which is idolatry. On account of these the wrath of God is coming. In these you too once walked, when you were living in them. But now you must put them all away: anger, wrath, malice, slander, and obscene talk from your mouth. Do not lie to one another, seeing that you have put off the old self with its practices and have put on the new self, which is being renewed in knowledge after the image of its creator." Notice how the imperative is grounded in the indicative. If you have been raised with Christ, *then* seek and set your minds on the things that are above. We need to do these things *because*

---

[109] See Moo, *Romans,* 390-91 and Schreiner, *Romans 321-22* for excellent reflections on this chapter and the indicative/imperative relationship.

(for) we have died and our life is hid with Christ. Because of this reality we must put to death what is earthly in us. We once walked in disobedience but now must put them away. That is, we must be obedient, *seeing that* we have put off the old self and put on the new self. Notice the gospel logic the apostle uses in this beautiful passage. The evangel brings an ethic.

Galatians 5:1and 5:25 also holds the indicative and the imperative in proper balance[110]: "For freedom Christ has set us free; stand firm therefore, and do not submit again to a yoke of slavery." In other words, "Christ has set us free, so be free." Verse 25 says, "If we live by the Spirit, let us also walk by the Spirit." I don't think Paul is using the verbs "live" and "walk" in a technical way here. He means, "If we live by the Spirit, let us live by the Spirit," or "If we walk in the Spirit, let us walk in the Spirit." The indicative grounds the imperative.

Philippians 2:12-13 is a popular verse showing that God's work is the cause of our work: "Therefore, my beloved, as you have always obeyed, so now, not only as in my presence but much more in my absence, work out your own salvation with fear and trembling, *for* it is God who works in you, both to will and to work for his good pleasure" (emphasis mine). God's work doesn't eliminate our work but is the basis for it. Our work is established and secured by God's work.[111]

---

[110] I owe much of this exegetical insight to Richard Gaffin, *By Faith, Not by Sight* (Waynesboro, GA: Paternoster, 2006), 70ff.

[111] Schreiner, *Paul*, 257.

This sort of gospel logic abounds in Paul's letters (see Rom 6:14, 7:4, 2 Corinthians 5:15, Gal 5:1, 1 Cor 15:10). Ephesians 5:8 encourages us by reminding us that though we were once in darkness, we are now light in the Lord. Paul then immediately exhorts us to walk as children of light. In other words, "Walk as children of light, because in the Lord, you are children of light. Colossians 3:9 says that we have put on the new self (indicative) while Ephesians 4:22 commands us to put on the new self (imperative). Galatians 3:27 says we who have been baptized into Christ have put on Christ (indicative), while Romans 13:14 commands us to put on the Lord Jesus Christ (imperative).

Brothers and sisters, before we think about our own obedience, we must keep this balance in mind. We have been justified by faith. Now we must pursue holiness, without which no one will see the Lord (Heb 12:14). Finally, we get to the question, what standard are we to be obedient to? What, or who, is the authority of the new covenant Christian?

PART II

THE LAW OF CHRIST

We will use 1 Corinthians 9:20-21 as a springboard for the discussion of the law of Christ. That verse reads, "To the Jews I became as a Jew, in order to win Jews. To those under the law I became as one under the law (though not being myself under the law) that I might win those under the law. To those outside the law I became as one outside the law (not being outside the law of God but under the law of Christ) that I might win those outside the law." In context Paul is discussing the nature of his own apostleship. Paul was the first great missionary theologian, willing and able to flex concerning the law so as not to be a stumbling block to any, and by all means save some. In his discussion, we gain insight to how we should think about the law. It is crystal clear that Paul does not see himself as under the authority of the Mosaic law. He also does not view the Mosaic law as God's law for the new covenant age. He sees himself as under the law of God, which is being under the law of Christ (in-lawed to Christ).

CHAPTER 3

THOUGH NOT BEING MYSELF
UNDER THE LAW

The first phrase to be discussed is clear from a number of New Testament passages. The New Testament writers view the Old Covenant (=Mosaic Covenant/ law covenant) as having passed away. It is *old*. It has been replaced by the New Covenant.

Recently, Jason Meyer has shown this definitively in my estimation in his recent book, *The End of the Law: Mosaic Covenant in Pauline Theology*.[112] Before entering the discussion of the old and new covenants, he lays out a very important structural consideration. Paul has several contrasts in his teachings: old covenant/new covenant, old age/new age, death/resurrection, law/gospel, futility/hope, decay/renewal, law/faith, sin/righteousness, slavery/freedom, flesh/Spirit, letter/Spirit, etc. But what is the structural foundation that undergirds these contrasts? Meyer follows the great Reformed biblical theologian

---

[112] Jason C. Meyer, *The End of the Law: Mosaic Covenant in Pauline Theology* (Nashville: B&H Academic, 2009). He writes that "new" in Paul's letters "is the eschatological counterpart of the 'old,' and thus 'newness' contains an element of the eschatological advance in Paul's theology. The 'new' entity accomplishes what the 'old' failed to do. Therefore, the 'new' also replaces the 'old'" (53). See also my, *The Newness of the New Covenant* (Frederick, MD: New Covenant Media, 2008).

Geerhardus Vos, who writes, "the comprehensive antitheses of the First Adam and the Last Adam, sin and righteousness, the flesh and the Spirit, law and faith, and these are precisely the historic reflections of the one great transcendental antithesis between this world and the world-to-come."[113] History is structured around the two Adams who represent the two ages. So the old covenant is old because it belongs to the old age, and as such is transitory, non-eschatological, and ineffectual.[114] Meyer writes, "Old things are qualitatively old because they belong to the old age. New things are qualitatively new because they belong to the new age."[115] Christ, the Last Adam, inaugurated the new covenant and new creation through his death and resurrection. The Last Adam "gave himself for our sins to deliver us from the present evil age" (Gal 1:4).

Gospels

The gospels are clear that the Mosaic law is no longer operative in the new age. Here are just a *few* examples[116]: In Matthew 17:24-27 Jesus teaches that the sons are free with regard to the temple tax. Though Lepers are to live alone outside the camp (Lev 13:45-46), in Mark 1:41 Jesus

---

[113] Geerhardus Vos, *The Pauline Eschatology* (Phillipsburg, NJ: P&R Publishing, 1994), 60-61.

[114] As Stephen Westerholm writes, "With or without the Sinaitic covenant, 'in Adam all die'," *Perspectives*, 363.

[115] Meyer, *The End of the Law*, 57.

[116] We will examine Matthew 5:17-48 in another section below.

cleanses a Leper by *touching* him.[117] Leviticus 15:25-27 teaches that if anyone touches a woman with a discharge of blood, they will become unclean, yet in Mark 5:24-34, Jesus healed the woman who had a discharge of blood for twelve years by being *touched* by her. Jesus reverses Leviticus 15: Jesus doesn't become unclean, but she becomes clean![118]

Circumcision, an old covenant requirement (Lev 12:3) is clearly no longer required. In the new covenant, circumcision is a matter of the heart by the Spirit, not outward and physical, by the letter (Rom 2:28-29, cf. Deut 30:6). Circumcision or uncircumcision counts for nothing, but faith working though love (Gal 5:6), the new creation (Gal 6:15), and keeping God's commands is everything (1 Cor 7:19). More will be said about the Sabbath below. The food laws of the Mosaic law (Deut 14:3-21, Lev 11:1-47, 20:25-26) are clearly no longer operative in the new age either. Jesus said, "It is not what goes into the mouth that defiles a person, but what comes out of the mouth; this defiles a person" (Matt 15:11). Mark fleshes this out a bit with his helpful and significant parenthetical statement "Thus he declared all foods clean" (Mark 7:19; cf Luke 11:41).[119] Jesus teaching is made explicit to Peter in the vision(s) of Acts 10-11. Peter sees a sheet from heaven with all kinds of animals. A voice from heaven tells him to eat,

---

[117] Thomas R. Schreiner, *40 Questions About the Law* (Grand Rapids: Kregel Academic, forthcoming), 185; idem, *New Testament Theology*, 618-19

[118] Ibid. Schreiner shows that Mark emphasizes that the woman touched Jesus by calling attention to it four times (vv. 27, 28, 30, 31)

[119] David Peterson, *Engaging With God: A Biblical Theology of Worship* (Downers Grove, IL: InterVarstiy Press, 1992), 114.

but he, being a good Jew refuses. Then the Lord said, "What God has made clean, do not call common" (10:15). David Peterson writes, "Peter must acknowledge God's right to determine what is clean and to redefine boundaries for the gospel era."[120] Paul can say, "I know and am persuaded in the Lord Jesus that nothing is unclean in itself" (Rom 14:14) and "everything is indeed clean" (Rom 14:20) but never cause a brother to stumble in what you eat (Rom 14:1-15:6).[121]

Paul

Believers in Christ are "not under law but under grace" (Rom 6:14). "Law" (*ho nomos*) in Paul's usage is most often referring to the Mosaic covenant.[122] Paul is referring to two

---

[120] David G. Peterson, *The Acts of the Apostles* The Pillar New Testament Commentary (Grand Rapids: Eerdmans, 2009), 330.

[121] Much more could said from the book of Acts. See the wonderful treatment by Craig L. Blomberg, "The Law in Luke-Acts," *Journal for the Study of the New Testament* 22 (October 1984): 53-80. I find it very interesting that Stephen is charged with speaking "blasphemous words against Moses" (6:11) and "This man never ceases to speak words against this holy place and the law" (6:13).

[122] Douglas Moo, "Paul and the Law in the Last Ten Years," Scottish Journal of Theology 40 (1987):287-307; idem, "Law, Works of Law, and Legalism in Paul," WTJ 45 (1983): 73-100; Seifrid, Christ, Our Righteousness, 96; Westerholm agrees: "law in Paul's letters "frequently (indeed, most frequently) refers to the sum of specific divine requirements given to Israel through Moses," Perspectives, 299. I think Paul does mean something like "principle" in Rom 3:27, contra Stanton, who takes it to be "the law discerned and obeyed on the basis of faith in Jesus. In other words, this phrase is a first cousin of ho nomos tou Christou," in "The Law of Christ: A Neglected Theological Gem?," 174. I also think that both uses of "law" in Rom

different salvation-historical powers.[123] He could have just as easily said, "We are not in the old age, but in the new."[124] He is referring to two different eras in salvation history. New covenant believers are no longer "bound by the demands of the Mosaic law code and subject to its sanctions."[125] It will not do to say that we are only free from *parts* of the law such as the civil or ceremonial but still under the moral law.[126] As New Testament scholar Stephen Westerholm writes, "Were that the case, however, Paul would have had to provide his churches with detailed instructions as to which commands they were obligated to observe and which they were not: this was obviously a very important matter! But there is no evidence that he made any such distinctions. On the contrary, it is clear that, for Paul, Torah was a unit."[127] Moreover, if Paul only meant we are free from the civil or ceremonial parts of the law, Romans 6:15 (What then? Are we to sin because we are not

---

8:2 are simply word plays (see Fee, God's Empowering Presence, 522).

[123] Moo, Romans, 389; Schreiner, Romans, 326; idem, New Testament Theology, 534, 647-48.

[124] Douglas J. Moo, "The Law of Christ as the Fulfillment of the Law of Moses: A Modified Lutheran View," in Five Views on Law and Gospel, ed. Stanley N. Gundry (Grand Rapids: Zondervan, 1999), 361, 366, 368.

[125] Westerholm, Perspectives, 300, 431-33; idem, "Letter and Spirit: The Foundation of Pauline Ethics," New Testament Studies 30 (1984): 242-43; Moo, "The Law of Moses or the Law of Christ," 211-12, 214.

[126] E.g. see Michael Horton, Introducing Covenant Theology (Grand Rapids: Baker, 2006), 177-80.

[127] Stephen Westerholm, "Letter and Spirit," 243; idem, Israel's Law and the Church's Faith (Grand Rapids: Eerdmans, 1988), 208.

under law but under grace?) would not be a legitimate objection to Paul's argument.[128]

Although this tripartite distinction is historically rooted and held by many men more respectable and learned[129] than the present writer, it must be rejected.[130] This distinction simply will not hold up to exegesis.[131] It is a theological construction imposed on the Text of Scripture. For Paul, to accept circumcision is to obligate oneself to keep the whole law (Gal 5:3). For James, to fail in one point of the law is to become accountable for all of it (Ja 2:10). Everything God demanded from Israel was moral. The law

---

[128] Westerholm, *Perspectives*, 432.

[129] For one great example, see Calvin, *Institutes*, 4.20.15, 1503-04.

[130] See the important and helpful article by David A. Dorsey, "The Law of Moses and the Christian: A Compromise," 321-334. He shows the impossibility of dividing up the law and the impossibility of believers obeying the law.

[131] Stephen Westerholm, "Law and Gospel in Jesus and Paul," in *Jesus and Paul Reconnected: Fresh Pathways into an Old Debate*, ed. Still, Todd D (Grand Rapids: Eerdmans, 2007), 32; Gary D. Long, *Biblical Law and Ethics: Absolute and Covenantal* (Frederick, MD: New Covenant Media, 2008), 53 n57, 87; John Reisinger, *In Defense of Jesus, the New Lawgiver*, (Frederick, MD: New Covenant Media, 2008), 209-229; idem, *Tablets of Stone*, 112-113, 117, 145; Schreiner, *40 questions*, 97-105; Moo, "The Law of Moses or the Law of Christ," 218; Seifrid, *Christ, Our Righteousness*, 63 n73; Meyer, *The End of the Law*, 282; Femi Adeyemi, "The New Covenant Law and the Law of Christ," *Bibliotheca Sacra* 163, no. 652 (October-December 2006), 445; Blomberg, "The Law in Luke-Acts," 69, who notes that Jesus challenges both moral and ritual law with his teaching on divorce and cleanliness and that the issues the Jerusalem council laid down were primarily *ritual matters*; the list could go on.

is a unit.[132] Observing the literary structure in Exodus bears this out.[133] Chapters 19 and 24 frame the "book of the covenant" (24:7). Chapter 19 gives the background. Chapter 24 describes the ceremony of covenant ratification. Verse one of chapter twenty introduces the ten words and 21:1 introduces the rules or ordinances of chapters 21-23. The rules of chapters 21-23 are applications of the ten words to specific social situations. Chapters 20 and 21-23 constitute specific sections of the covenant that *cannot be separated.* Gentry writes, "One cannot take the Ten Commandments as "eternal" and the Ordinances as "temporal" for both sections together constitute the agreement or covenant made between God and Israel."[134] Gentry writes, "It is common to categorize and classify the laws as (a) moral, (b) civil, and (c) ceremonial, but this classification is foreign to the material and imposed upon it from the outside rather than arising from the material and being clearly marked by the literary structure of text."[135] The law constitutes the stipulations of the covenant, and both have passed away with the coming of Christ.[136]

---

[132] Seifrid, *Christ, Our Righteousness,* 97, 102, 123.

[133] See Peter J. Gentry, "The Covenant at Sinai," *The Southern Baptist Journal of Theology* 12, no. 3 (Fall 2008): 38-63, for which this section is indebted.

[134] Gentry, "The Covenant at Sinai," 60.

[135] Ibid.

[136] Some point to Rom 3:31 to argue that the law has not ceased: "Do we then overthrow the law by this faith? By no means! On the contrary, we uphold the law." This cannot mean that the Law is still our authority in the new covenant. If it did, we better get busy cutting foreskins and slicing goats (see Moo, "The Law of Christ as the Fulfillment of the Law of Moses," 371). It seems to me that this short

assertion has two possible interpretations. One option is to see the
true nature and purpose of the law as coming to light when viewed
from the perspective of justification by faith (Westerholm,
Perspectives, 322 n80). Moo links 3:31 with 8:4 to show that
"Justification takes full account of the law, providing for its
complete satisfaction in believers through their incorporation into
Christ," "The Law of Christ as the Fulfillment of the Law of Moses,"
372; idem, *Romans*, 255, 484. In this view, the law finds its true
purpose, not in justifying sinners, but in bringing the knowledge of
sin (cf. Rom 3:20, 7:7). In my opinion, the second option is more
likely what Paul has in mind, namely, we uphold the law (i.e. the
law and the prophets – the Scriptures) in its witnessing function to
the righteousness of God. The law is still authoritative in its
prophetic witness to Christ in his saving work. In Rom 3:21, the
Law and the Prophets bear witness to the righteousness of God.
And it cannot be overlooked that Rom 3:31 is a transition to chapter
four where Paul will show how the law and prophets did so with
the Abraham narrative. So Rom 4:3 asks, "For what does the
Scripture say? Abraham believed God, and it was counted to him as
righteousness." Others point to 1 Tim 1:8-10 to refute the position
argued for in this section: "Now we know that the law is good, if
one uses it lawfully, understanding this, that he law is not laid
down for the just but for the lawless and disobedient, for the
ungodly and sinners, for the unholy and profane, for those who
strike their fathers and mothers, for murderers, the sexually
immoral, men who practice homosexuality, enslavers, liars,
perjurers, and whatever else is contrary to sound doctrine." But this
verse is clear that the law is not to be used as the standard for
believers. There was obviously a problem with people who desired
to be teachers of the law (1:7). What is interesting is these teachers
were probably only teaching the "moral" aspects of the law since
there is no mention of circumcision. Paul is clear that the law is not
for Christians (the just) but for sinners though he does not spell out
what function the law performs among them. See Stephen
Westerholm, "The Law and the 'Just Man' (1 Tim 1,3-11)," *Studia
Theolgica* 36 (1982); Moo, "The Law of Moses or the Law of Christ,"
216.

Galatians could not be clearer on its insistence that believers are no longer bound to the Mosaic Covenant. In this precious letter, Paul "argues so vigorously that those who continue to follow the path marked out by the Mosaic Law are under the Law's curse that he must address his readers' inevitable question, 'Why then the law?' (Gal 3:19)."[137] All who are of the works of the law are under a curse (3:10), but Christ has redeemed us from the curse of the law by becoming a curse for us (3:13). The law had a definite historical starting point: 430 years after Abraham was given the promise (Gen 12:1-3). The law, which was given later, "does not annul a covenant previously ratified by God, so as to make the promise void. For if the inheritance comes by the law, it no longer comes by promise; but God gave it to Abraham by a promise" (3:17-18).

In answering the inevitable question, "Why then the law," Paul no doubt shocks his readers when he says it was added to increase sin (*tōn parabaseōn charin* 3:19, cf. Rom 5:20, Exod 32:7-8)![138] The Jewish mantra was the more law

---

[137] Frank Thielman, "Law and Liberty in the Ethics of Paul," *Ex Auditu* 11 (1995): 64.

[138] Thomas R. Schreiner, *Galatians*, Zondervan Exegetical Commentary (Grand Rapids: Zondervan, forthcoming), 204; Westerholm, *Perspectives*, 426; Graham Stanton, "The Law of Moses and the Law of Christ," in *Paul and the Mosaic Law*, ed. Dunn, James D.G (Grand Rapids: Eerdmans, 1996), 112; Meyer, *The End of the Law*, 168-70; Moo, "The Law of Christ as the Fulfillment of the Law of Moses," 340-41. Hence, Luther was thoroughly Pauline when he wrote, "The law of God, the most salutary doctrine of life, cannot advance man on his way to righteousness, but rather hinders him," "Heidelberg Disputation," in *Martin Luther's Basic Theological Writings*, 30.

the more life, not the more law the more transgression. Paul was not concerned with winning friends and influencing people but with showing the significance of the person and work of Jesus Christ. Just as we saw that the law had a definite starting point (430 years after the promise to Abraham), Galatians also teaches that it has a definite ending point: the arrival of the Messiah. The law was added _until_ the offspring should come to whom the promise had been made (3:19), _until_ the coming faith would be revealed (3:23), _until_ Christ came (3:24).

The law was our guardian or pedagogue (_paidagōgos_) until Christ came (Gal 3:24). The word _guardian_ used here is important. The King James Version's rendering of this word as _schoolmaster_, or the New American Standard's _tutor_ are not helpful, for, as Richard Longenecker has pointed out, "While today we think of pedagogues as teachers, in antiquity a _paidagōgos_ was distinguished from a _didaskalos_ ('teacher') and had custodial and disciplinary functions rather than educative or instructional ones."[139] In ancient Greco-Roman society, the _paidagōgos_ was a domestic slave within the household who was responsible for supervising the children from infancy to late adolescence.[140] _Paidagōgos_

[139] Richard N. Longenecker, _Galatians_, WBC 41 (Dallas: Word, 1990), 146; idem, "The Pedagogical Nature of the Law in Galatians 3:19-4:7," _Journal of the Evangelical Theological Society_ 25.1 (1982): 53; Cf. also BDAG 3rd ed., 748.

[140] Ibid., 148. Also see Linda L. Belleville, "'Under Law': Structural Analysis and the Pauline Concept of Law in Galatians 3.21-4.11," _Journal for the Study of the New Testament_ 26 (1986): 59; Frank Thielman, _Paul and the Law_ (Downers Grove, IL: InterVarsity Press, 1994), 132;.

is probably best translated "babysitter,"[141] or "nanny" in this context, as Paul clearly uses the term to refer to the law-covenant's temporal nature.[142] Nannies are only needed until maturity was reached, then they became unnecessary. The law covenant was, *by divine design*, temporary.[143] It was a parenthesis in redemptive history.[144] Believers are not children of the slave woman Hagar, who is Sinai, but children of Sarah the free woman and the Jerusalem above is our mother (Gal 4:21-31).

Under the Elemental Spirits

The word *under* (*hypo*) is used frequently in Galatians to refer to the old age. It designates "the old era when the

---

[141] Schreiner, *New Testament Theology*, 366, 534, 646; idem, "The Commands of God," 83; Douglas Moo, "The Law of Christ as the Fulfillment of the Law of Moses: A Modified Lutheran View," in *Five Views on Law and Gospel*, ed. Gundry, Stanley N (Grand Rapids: Zondervan, 1999), 338; N.T. Wright, *Paul* (Minneapolis: Fortress Press, 2009), 97; Meyer, *The End of the Law*, 173 n191.

[142] Stanton, "The Law of Moses and the Law of Christ," 114. Moo, "The Law of Moses or the Law of Christ," 214; Thielman, *Paul and the Law*, 133; idem, "Law and Liberty," 65; Schreiner, *Paul*, 128-30; idem, *Law and Its Fulfillment*, 78-80; Seifrid, *Christ, Our Righteousness*, 108.

[143] Westerholm, *Perspectives*, 330. This is an important point to make. God *intended* that the old covenant would be temporary and ineffective. It is not the case that God had to resort to plan B. The law is not opposed to the promises in the plan of God (Gal 3:21). The Mosaic covenant, *not the church*, is the parenthesis in the one plan of God centered in Jesus Christ (Eph 1:9-10). His eternal purpose was to make known his manifold wisdom to the rulers and authorities in the heavenly places *through the church* (Eph 3:10).

[144] Moo, "The Law of Christ as the Fulfillment of the Law of Moses," 361.

Mosaic covenant was in force."[145] In Galatians, to be under law (3:23) = under sin (3:22) = under a babysitter (3:25) = under guardians and managers (4:2) = under the elemental spirits (*stoicheia*) of the world (4:3).[146] This last one is the most shocking. The phrase I have translated "elemental spirits" is much disputed.[147] The ESV translates the word *elementary principles* here but translates the same word "elemental spirits" in Colossians 2:8 and 2:20. Many commentators take it to mean the physical building blocks of the world, so that to return to the law is to return to live under the basic principles of the world (most likely the case in 2 Pet 3:10, 12).[148] This may be a correct interpretation, but in the end, spiritual forces can't be excluded. For, unlike the mindset of Enlightenment rationalism, in the mindset of the New Testament, the "whole world lies in the power of the evil one" (1 John 5:19). Satan is the "god of this world" (2 Cor 4:4). He is the "ruler of this world" (John 12:31). Unbelievers follow "the prince of the power of the air" (Eph 2:2). There are cosmic powers, spiritual forces of evil over this present darkness (Eph 6:12).[149] So even if the

---

[145] Schreiner, *Paul*, 321

[146] The ESV curiously leaves out *hypo* here, opting for "were enslaved to the elementary principles of the world," missing the word's importance in this section. The TNIV is better here: "we were in slavery under the elemental spiritual forces of the world."

[147] See the discussion in Douglas J. Moo, *The Letters to the Colossians and to Philemon*, PNTC (Grand Rapids: Eerdmans, 2008), 187-93; Longenecker, *Galatians*, 165-66.

[148] Longenecker, *Galatians*, 166.

[149] Lest I be misunderstood, it should be noted that though Satan and his minions "rule" over this present evil age, *ultimately* their rule serves divine purposes. As Luther said, the devil is God's devil.

word does refer to the elementary building blocks of the world, demonic forces are still involved.

Some object to this interpretation (i.e. elemental sprits or spiritual forces) due to the claim that this usage is not used outside the Bible until after the second century A.D. Although looking at usage outside of the New Testament is helpful, it is not decisive. Usage in context is key.[150] In Galatians, Paul uses the word in 4:3 and 4:9. In 4:8-10, he writes, "Formerly, when you did not know God, you were enslaved to those that by nature are not gods. But now that you have come to know God, or rather to be known by God, how can you turn back again to the weak and worthless elementary principles [or elemental spirits] of the world, whose slaves you want to be once more? You observe days and months and seasons and years!" This is a shocking statement. Here Paul lumps together Judaism and paganism. To observe the Jewish Sabbath and festival practices (certainly this is what's in view) is to return to the elemental spirits of the world.[151] The genitive "of the world" (*tou kosmou*) is important as well. These elemental spirits are characteristic of this world, this age, which he already wrote is evil (Gal 1:4). This present world order belongs to Satan (2 Cor 4:4)

We are helped in our understanding of this truth by looking at the book of 1 Corinthians. There, referring to idols, Paul says "there may be so-called gods in heaven or

---

[150] D.G. Reid, "Elements/Elemental Spirits of the World," in *Dictionary of Paul and His Letters,* ed. Gerald F. Hawthorne, et al. (Downers Grove, IL: InterVarsity Press, 1993), 229.

[151] Westerholm, *Perspectives,* 367; Schreiner, *Galatians,* 245; Longenecker, *Galatians,* 182; Meyer, *The End of the Law,* 174.

on earth – as indeed there are many 'gods' and many 'lords'" (8:5). Then in 10:20 he says that these idols are demons: "No, I imply that what pagans sacrifice they offer to demons and not to God." So for the Galatians to return to the Jewish calendar is to return to being enslaved to those that are by nature not gods, which is another way of saying being enslaved by the elemental spirits of this present evil age. Clinton Arnold writes, "The passage is best explained if one interprets the *stoicheia* as demonic powers, equivalent to the expression 'principalities and powers.'[152] It's important to note that Paul is not calling the law demonic. However, it is demonic to return to the law *after* Christ's death and resurrection.[153] Christ is the end of the law. Its sacrifices are no longer effective. To turn back the clock of redemptive history is to turn to slavery to the powers.

If my interpretation is correct, it just reinforces the fact that getting the gospel right is crucial. The indicative

---

[152] Clinton E. Arnold, "Returning to the Domain of the Powers: *stoicheia* as Evil Spirits in Galatians 4:3, 9," *Novum Testamentum* 38, no. 1 (January 1996): 57; idem, *Powers of Darkness: Principalities and Powers in Paul's Letters* (Downers Grove, IL: InteVarsity Press, 1992), 53, 131-32.

[153] Richard Longenecker writes that Paul's use of the adverbs anew and again in Gal 4:9 "emphasizes the fact that by taking on Torah observance Gentile Christians would be reverting to a pre-Christian stance comparable to their former pagan worship...not, of course, that paganism and the Mosaic law are qualitatively the same, but that both fall under the same judgment when seen from the perspective of being 'in Christ' and that both come under the same condemnation when favored above Christ. Beyond question, Paul's lumping of Judaism and paganism together in this manner is radical in the extreme," *Galatians*, 181.

undergirds the imperative. Sanctification flows from justification. It is fundamentally demonic to trust in anything but Christ crucified for salvation. This is why John can call those who falsely claim to be Jews the synagogue of Satan (Rev 2:9, 3:9). In this regard the principalities and powers, the lords that cannot liberate,[154] can equally plunder the Roman Catholic Church or the overly strict fundamentalist Baptist congregation. The "do this and live" principle is everywhere because the main evangelist of this religion is the prince of the power of the air. Only pagans trust in self.[155] In Acts 21:24, the verbal form (*stoicheō*) is used of "live in observance of the law." It refers to "leading a closely regulated life, to living according to definite rules."[156] In Colossae, there were intruders trying to force the Colossians to live a certain way with regard to food, drink, festivals and Sabbaths (2:16). They were insisting on asceticism (2:18). But we have died to the law (Rom 7:4) and have died to the elemental spirits of the world (Col 2:20) and are no longer required to "submit to regulations – Do not handle, Do not taste, Do not touch" (2:20-21). Verlyn Verbrugge writes, "Thus 'the basic principles of the world' cover all the things in which

---

[154] Horton, The Gospel-Driven Life, 195.

[155] Schreiner writes, "Idolatry is the fundamental sin because self rather than God becomes the center of one's affections and reliance. Faith is the only way to please God because it looks to him as the all-sufficient one," Romans, 739.

[156] Verlyn D. Verbrugge, ed., New International Dictionary of New Testament Theology: Abridged Edition (Grand Rapids: Zondervan, 2000), 541.

humans place trust apart from the living God revealed in Christ."[157]

This perspective is also clear from Philippians 3:2. The Judaizers were very concerned about being ceremonially clean, doing good, and being circumcised and Paul provocatively calls them dogs (unclean), evil doers (opposite of good), and those who mutilate the flesh (*tēn katatōmēn*). There is a word play at work here on the word *circumcision* (*peritōmē*). He is saying that those who cut themselves thinking this will gain salvation are "like the frenzied prophets of Baal who were frustrated that their god would not answer their pleas" (see 1 Kin 18:28, Lev 19:28, 21:5 LXX).[158] Paul tells those who would force Christians to be circumcised that they should go ahead and lop the whole thing off (*apokoptō*) (Gal 5:12), with the result that they will not be able to enter the church of the Lord (Deut 23:1, 2 LXX - *apokoptō*)!

---

[157] Ibid. Longenecker writes similarly, "For Paul, however, whatever leads one away from sole reliance on Christ, whether based on good intentions or depraved desires, is sub-Christian and therefore to be condemned," *Galatians*, 181.

[158] Thielman, *Theology of the New Testament*, 318.

CHAPTER 4

NOT UNDER THE LAW PART 2

Back to Paul

In Romans 7:4-6, we read that believers have died to the law through the body of Christ and have been "released from the law, having died to that which held us captive, so that we serve in the new way of the Spirit and not in the old way of the written code" (cf. Gal 2:19). Written code is literally translated "letter" (*grammatos*), and clearly refers to the Mosaic Law (cf. 2 Cor 3:6). Earlier in Romans, he had written, "For no one is a Jew who is merely one outwardly, nor is circumcision outward and physical. But a Jew is one inwardly, and circumcision is a matter of the heart, by the Spirit, not by the letter" (2:28-29). First in this verse we see that Dispensationalism is implausible, but that is another book. Second and for our purposes, we see another salvation-historical contrast. Letter = old age/old covenant. Spirit = new age/new covenant.[159]

Ephesians 2:14-15 says, "For he himself is our peace, who has made us both one and has broken down in his flesh the dividing wall of hostility by abolishing the law of

---

[159] Moo writes that the letter/Spirit antithesis is "between the Old Covenant and the New, the old age and the new," in *Romans*, 421. Seifrid writes that letter is "best understood as a reference to the will of God in their form of written demands. 'Letter" and 'Spirit" represent two different ways in which God addresses the human being," *Christ, Our Righteousness*, 98.

commandments and ordinances, that he might create in himself one new man in place of the two." On the cross, Christ abolished (*katargeō*) the law.[160] Paul doesn't say the civil and ceremonial parts, but the law of commandments expressed in ordinances. If Paul expected the Ephesians to continue to uphold the moral aspects of this law, he would have had to have said more than this. In Romans 10:4 says, "For Christ is the end of the law for righteousness to everyone who believes." The word *end* (*telos*) is best translated "culmination" because Christ is both the goal (teleological) and end (temporal) of the Mosaic law. Moo writes, "He is its 'goal,' in the sense that the law has always anticipated and looked forward to Christ. But he is also its 'end' in that his fulfillment of the law brings to an end that period of time when it was a key element in the plan of God."[161]

In 2 Corinthians 3:7 the apostle Paul, under the inspiration of the Holy Spirit, called the old covenant a "ministry of death" (cf. Deut 30:15, 19). The letter kills but the Spirit gives life. The tablets of stone were ineffective. They didn't get the job done. Humanity in Adam is not altered by the old covenant. It had glory, but now its glory

---

[160] Hal Harless, "The Cessation of the Mosaic Covenant," *Bibliotheca Sacra* 160 (July-September 2003): 36-61; Long, *Biblical Law and Ethics,* 27. O'Brien writes, "What is abolished is the 'law-covenant,' that is, the law as a whole conceived as a covenant. It is then replaced by a new covenant for Jews *and* Gentiles," *Ephesians,* 199.

[161] Moo, "The Law of Moses or the Law of Christ," 207; idem, *Romans,* 641 where he uses the analogy of a race course. The finish line is both the termination of the race, and the goal of the race; idem, "The Law of Christ as the Fulfillment of the Law of Moses," 358; Meyer, *The End of the Law,* 212; Schreiner, *New Testament Theology,* 532.

"was being brought to an end" (2 Cor 3:7, 13). The new covenant ministry of the Spirit has much more glory than the old covenant ministry of the letter (3:7-11). The old covenant functions like a candle when one loses their electricity. It is needed until the power returns, but once the power returns, the candle pales in comparison to the three lamps in the living room. The candle served its purpose and is now put back where it belongs. Jason Meyer writes, "The contrast between the old covenant and the new covenant is between something being brought to an end and something that will endure. In other words, Paul presents this eschatological contrast in terms of impermanence and permanence. Paul can affirm both the glory of the old covenant and the termination of the old covenant and its glory because of the eschatological arrival of the new covenant."[162]

If the above formulation of what it means to be free from the law is accused of being antinomian, then I believe we stand in good company. After all, it was not me or any other New Covenant Theologian who said we are not under law. It was Christ and his Apostles.

The Gift of the Spirit

We see from Romans 2:28-29, 7:1-6, 2 Corinthians 3, and many other passages that "the Spirit serves for Paul as the essential element of the new covenant."[163] The old covenant was inadequate in part because it lacked the Spirit. It issued commands but provided no power to obey. So

---

[162] Meyer, *The End of the Law*, 93.

[163] Gordon D. Fee, *God's Empowering Presence: The Holy Spirit in the Letters of Paul* (Peabody, MA: Hendrickson Publishers, 1994), 508.

Luther writes, "For by the Law Moses can do no more than tell what men ought to do and not do. However he does not provide the strength and ability for such doing and not doing, and thus lets us stick in sin."[164] As John Reisinger has said, "the Old Covenant carried a footnote that said, 'Batteries not included.' The New Covenant remedies that deficiency by the gift of the Holy Spirit."[165] In reflecting on the new covenant, and on carrying out the law of Christ, the role of the empowering presence of the Spirit cannot be emphasized enough.

The prophets foretold of a coming new covenant/new age/new exodus/new creation that would be characterized by the Messiah and the Spirit. New Testament scholar Max Turner writes, "The future was thus to be an epoch characterized by the lavish outpouring of God's Spirit."[166] The Lord, through Jeremiah, spoke of a day when he would make a new covenant with his people (31:31).[167] It will not be like the Mosaic covenant (31:32). This bears repeating: It will not be like the Mosaic covenant. It seems clear to me that the Lord means a new covenant, not a renewed covenant. *Covenant Theologian* (you read me right) Michael Horton writes, "The point could not be clearer: the new covenant is not a renewal of the old covenant made at Sinai, but an entirely different covenant with an entirely

---

[164] Luther, "Preface to the Old Testament," 125.

[165] John G. Reisinger, *But I Say Unto You* (Frederick, MD: New Covenant Media, 2006), 14.

[166] Max Turner, *The Holy Spirit and Spiritual Gifts* (Peabody, MA: Hendrickson Publishers, 1996), 6.

[167] Jeremiah 32:40 calls this an everlasting covenant.

different basis."[168] The Lord will put his law within his people, and write it on their hearts, and he will be their God and they his people (31:33). All within the covenant community will know the Lord (31:34)[169] and there will be full and final forgiveness (31:34).

Isaiah spoke of a coming Servant who would uniquely bear the Spirit (11:1-2, 42:1, 61:1). But this Messiah will not be the only bearer of the Spirit; Isaiah 32:15 says that the Spirit will be poured out upon us, and when the Spirit is poured out, the new creation will come: the wilderness becomes a fruitful field.[170] Isaiah 44:3 says, "For I will pour water on the thirsty land, and streams on the dry ground; I will pour my Spirit upon your offspring, and my blessing on your descendants." Since Isaiah 44:3 mentions both blessing and the Spirit, Paul is probably alluding to this passage when he writes that the *blessing* of Abraham (Gen 12:1-3) is the promised *Spirit* (Gal 3:14).[171] Both Ezekiel (39:29) and Joel (2:28-29) also promise a day when the Lord will pour out his Spirit. Joel writes, "And it shall come to pass afterward, that I will pour out my Spirit on all flesh" (2:28a). One of the key distinctives of the new covenant is that the Spirit will no longer be limited to certain prophets,

---

[168] Horton, *Introducing Covenant Theology*, 53, cf. 55, 69, 75, 101, 134.

[169] My anachronistic, theological paraphrase: The people of God will shift from a Presbyterian ecclesiology (mixed community) to a Baptist ecclesiology (regenerate community).

[170] Barry G. Webb, *The Message of Isaiah* (Downers Grove, IL: InterVarsity Press, 1996), 138-39; J. Alec Motyer, *The Prophecy of Isaiah* (Downers Grove, IL: InterVarsity Press, 1993), 260; Fee, *God's Empowering Presence*, 910.

[171] Schreiner, *Galatians*, 184.

priests, and kings, but everyone in the covenant community will have the Spirit.[172]

Ezekiel 11:19-20 says, "And I will give them one heart, and a new spirit I will put within them. I will remove the heart of stone from their flesh and give them a heart of flesh, that they may walk in my statutes and keep my rules and obey them. And they shall be my people, and I will be their God." The new covenant, the covenant of peace, the everlasting covenant will provide the power to obey: the Spirit of God himself. Ezekiel 36:25-27 is another very important text: "I will sprinkle clean water on you, and you shall be clean from all your uncleannesses, and from all your idols I will cleanse you. And I will give you a new heart, and a new spirit I will put within you. And I will remove the heart of stone from your flesh and give you a heart of flesh. And I will put my Spirit within you, and cause you to walk in my statutes and be careful to obey my rules." There can be no doubt that this passage, along with Jeremiah 31, informs Paul's discussion mentioned above in 2 Corinthians 3. The letter kills because it "has no batteries." But the Spirit gives life. Gordon Fee writes, "It is in this sense that 'the letter kills,' because it can arouse sin but is powerless to overcome it; the Torah lacks the one essential ingredient for life, the Spirit."[173] Ezekiel has a vision of a valley of dry bones that the Lord breathes life into and raises from the dead. Of course at this point in redemptive history, only one Israelite has been raised from the dead with the fullness of the Spirit, but he is the first

[172] D.A Carson, _Showing the Spirit_ (Grand Rapids: Baker Books, 1987), 152-53.

[173] Fee, _God's Empowering Presence,_ 306.

fruits, guaranteeing the rest of the harvest. When Paul, in 2 Corinthians 3:6, says that the Spirit gives life, surely he has Ezekiel 37:14 in mind: "And I will put my Spirit within you, and you shall live (see LXX)."[174]

These promises of the end-time gift of the Spirit were fulfilled at Pentecost (Acts 2). The Spirit is the evidence that the future is now, and is the guarantee that the kingdom will in fact be consummated.[175] As we will see, the believer in this age is not without need of exhortation. However, this fact ought not diminish the central role of the Spirit in the new covenant. We are called to walk by the Spirit (Gal 5:16), be led by the Spirit (5:18), live and keep in step with the Spirit (5:25), sow to the Spirit (6:8). By the Spirit, we are to put to death the deeds of the body (Rom 8:13). The Spirit is our "pedagogue" in the new covenant.[176] Doug Moo writes, "It is difficult to avoid the conclusion, then, that life in the Spirit is put forward by Paul as the ground of Christian ethics, *in contrast to* life 'under law'."[177]

Hebrews

The author of Hebrews agrees whole-heartedly with Paul. The old covenant has been replaced by the new. Hebrews 7:11 and 7:18 are clear that the law made nothing perfect due to its weakness and uselessness. A new

---

174 Ibid., 52.

175 Gordon D. Fee, Paul, the Spirit, and the People of God (Peabody, MA: Hendrickson Publishers, 1996), ix, xv, 2, 4, 53ff, 64, 146, 177, 181.

176 John G. Reisinger, *Tablets of Stone & the History of Redemption* (Frederick, MD: New Covenant Media, 2004), 104; idem, *But I Say Unto You*, 14, 77, 142.

177 Moo, "The Law of Moses or the Law of Christ," 215.

priesthood (Melchizedekian rather than Levitical) brings with it a new law (Heb 7:12). In chapter eight, the author includes the longest Old Testament quotation in the New when he quotes Jeremiah 31:31-34. Before doing so, he writes, "...Christ has obtained a ministry that is as much more excellent than the old as the covenant he mediates is better, since it is enacted on better promises. For if that first covenant had been faultless, there would have been no occasion to look for a second" (Heb 8:6-7). Right after the new covenant quotation we read, "In speaking of a new covenant, he makes the first one obsolete.[178] And what is becoming obsolete and growing old is ready to vanish away" (Heb 8:13). Eugene Peterson's Bible paraphrase *The Message* gets to the heart of what Hebrews 8:13 is saying: "By coming up with a new plan, a new covenant between God and his people, God put the old plan on the shelf. And there it stays, gathering dust."

---

[178] Here he uses this same word "obsolete" (*palaioo*) in Heb 1:11 where it refers to a garment wearing out. The language could not be any clearer. It has lost its usefulness.

CHAPTER 5

NOT BEING OUTSIDE THE LAW OF GOD

In 1 Corinthians 9:21, we read, "To those outside the law I became as one outside the law (not being outside the law of God but under the law of Christ) that I might win those outside the law." In saying that believers are free from the Mosaic law covenant, Paul is not saying that believers are completely free from any and all types of "law," if by that we mean commandments in general.[179] Christian freedom is not the equivalent of individual autonomy! New covenant believers are not lawless (*anamois*), in the sense of living however we like. Paul clearly distinguishes the commands of God in the new covenant from the commands of God in the old covenant in 1 Corinthians 7:19: "For neither circumcision counts for anything nor uncircumcision, but keeping the commandments of God." This, along with 1 Corinthians 9:20-21, is very insightful

---

[179] Commenting on Romans 6:14, Moo writes, "We are justified in considering the Christian to be free from the commandments of the Mosaic law insofar as they are part of that system, and perhaps in the sense that whatever commandments are applicable to us come with a new empowering through the 'indicative' of God's grace in Christ. But we cannot conclude from this verse that the believer has no obligation to any of the individual commandments of that law – insofar, we may say, as they may be isolated from the 'system.' Still less does this verse allow the conclusion that Christians are no longer subject to 'law' or 'commandments' at all – for *nomos* here means *Mosaic* law, not law' as such," *Romans*, 390; cf. 816-17, 817n39.

and important for the argument of this book. Paul is clearly not under the law covenant (7:19, 9:20), but he is still under the law of God (9:21) = the commandments of God (7:19) = the law of Christ (9:21). Circumcision, which *was* a commandment in the Mosaic law, is clearly not a commandment of God in the new covenant.[180]

It is also not the case that the Spirit has replaced all law (or commandments) and now one only needs to be led by the Spirit, left to subjectivism. One gets this impression from Gordon Fee's work. He writes, "This list of Spiritual fruit [Gal 5:22f] is *not* intended to regulate Christian behavior by rules of conduct. Because truly Christian ethics are the product of walking and living in the Spirit, there can be no law (Gal 5:23); nor may we turn Paul's ethics into a new law."[181] While believers are freed from the Mosaic

---

[180] D.A Carson writes, "The average first-century Jew would have said, 'Wait a minute! Circumcision *is* one of God's commands. How can you say that circumcision is nothing, and then immediately comment, 'Keeping God's commands is what counts?' The only answer is that, for Paul, the commands of God that he finds operative for the Christian cannot be equated with the Mosaic Code," *The Cross and Christian Ministry* (Grand Rapids, MI: Baker Books, 1993), 119.

[181] Fee, *Paul, the Spirit, and the People of God*, 115. Similarly, Westerholm writes, "The fact that, whereas the will of God for the Jew was found in the statutes of Torah, the Christian must discover it for himself as his mind is 'renewed' and he grows in 'insight' shows clearly that the will of God is no longer defined as an obligation to fulfill the law," in "Letter and Spirit," 243. While this is partly true, surely an honest reading of the New Testament reveals that believers are left with more than discovering God's will for ourselves. So also Westerholm, *Israel's Law*, 209. However, Westerholm goes on to say that we still need instruction as long as

law, one need not conclude that believers are free from all and any commandments. This is an over-realized eschatology. While we will need no moral exhortation[182] on the new earth, we are not there yet. Frank Thielman, in an excellent article on Pauline ethics, is worth quoting at length on this point:

> As long as believers, whose minds God has renewed, live in this age, they must strive not to be conformed to it. Paul therefore handed down to his churches a set body of moral teaching which provided a rough outline of what the Christian should look like who had been transformed by God. Although the time had come when God had poured out his Spirit on believers and transformed their hearts, it was still possible not to live by the Spirit, to allow the present evil age such latitude that an outside observer might not know the difference between the believer and the unbeliever (1 Cor 1:20; 2:6 8; 3:18; 5:1)…With the death and resurrection of Jesus and the outpouring of God's Spirit, the new age predicted by the prophets had dawned. The Mosaic Law was now obsolete and the Spirit enabled every believer to discern the will of God. But the "evil age" continues to be "present" and often obscures the believer's moral vision (Gal 1:4; cf. Rom 12:2; 1 Cor 3:18; 2 Tim 4:10). In such cases, the traditional moral teaching of the church, which Paul apparently handed down to his congregations as part of his gospel, remained necessary.[183]

---

we are still in the flesh, "Letter and Spirit," 245. See Calvin's response to the Anabaptists claiming they only needed the Spirit, *Institutes* 3.3.14, 606.

[182] Often called *paranesis*.

[183] Thielman, "Law and Liberty," 71-72. Similarly, Moo writes, "Christians often fail to walk in accordance with that Spirit and

78

The Spirit and moral exhortation are not at odds. Rather the Spirit uses moral exhortation to conform us to Christ. Guidance for the Christian has both internal (Spirit) and external (exhortation) aspects.[184]

For example, in Galatians gentleness is a fruit of the Spirit in 5:23 but this is not at odds with the command to restore (imperative) a brother in a spirit of *gentleness* (6:1). Here (again!) it is so important to keep the relationship of the indicative and the imperative in biblical balance. We have a right standing with God through Christ (indicative), and now we are to live in obedience to his Word (imperative).[185] New Covenant believers are not *anamois*! The New Testament is filled with commands and exhortations to live in light of the gospel of Jesus Christ. We do not yet fully walk in line with the Spirit and so need

---

need 'law' to correct and discipline them (Luther is eloquent on this point). But any approach that substitutes external commands for the Spirit as the basic norm for Christian living runs into serious difficulties with Paul," "The Law of Moses or the Law of Christ," 218; Schreiner, *New Testament Theology*, 655-56.

[184] Richard N. Longenecker, *Paul: Apostle of Liberty* (New York: Harper and Row Publishers, 1964), 190. Reisinger, *But I Say Unto You*, 144-45.

[185] Victor Paul Furnish, *Theology and Ethics in Paul* (Nashville: Abingdon, 1968), 224-27; Schreiner, *New Testament Theology*, 656-57. Mark Seifrid writes, Paul's "exhortation is invariably based upon the announcement of the salvation which God has worked in Christ. In short, where imperatives appear in Paul's letters, they appear in the form of gospel, in which the law has been taken up and transcended," *Christ, Our Righteousness*, 126-27; Meyer, *The End of the Law*, 280-81.

moral exhortation to "control the flesh."[186] Jesus gives a new *commandment* (John 13:34). To love Jesus is to keep his *commandments* (John 14:15, 21). Apollos "had been instructed in the way of the Lord" (Acts 18:25). As shown above, the epistles are full of imperatives (e.g. Rom 6-8). Just as we received Christ Jesus, we are to walk in him (Col 2:6). Believers are to avoid sensuality, greed, and every kind of impurity because "that is not the way you learned Christ" (Eph 4:20)![187] The Thessalonians were to aspire to live quietly, mind their own affairs, to work with their own hands, just as the Apostles had *instructed* them to do (1 Thess 4:11). In 1 Thessalonians 4:2-6, Paul reminds them about the *instruction* they had given them through the Lord Jesus, then lays out the will of God, not by citing the Torah, but by laying down apostolic commands (abstain, control, not transgress and wrong, etc). The new covenant church was doctrinally and *morally* instructed by Jesus and the apostles.

---

[186] Martin Luther, "Preface to the Old Testament," in *Martin Luther's Basic Theological Writings*, ed. Timothy F. Lull (Minneapolis: Fortress Press, 1989), 119.

[187] Peter T. O'Brien, writes, "Here in Ephesians Christ himself is the content of the teaching which the readers learned…This formulation signifies that when the readers accepted Christ as Lord, they not only welcomed him into their lives but also received traditional instruction about him…Learning Christ means welcoming him as a living person and being shaped by his teaching. This involves submitting to his rule of righteousness and responding to his summons to standards and values completely different from what they have known," *The Letter to the Ephesians* (Grand Rapids: Eerdmans, 1999), 324.

As Thielman noted above, the Apostles handed down traditional moral teaching (1 Thess 2:13, 2 Thess 2:15, 1 Cor 15:2, 1 Tim 6:20, 2 Tim 1:14, 1 Cor 11:2). Second Thessalonians is clear in this regard: "Now we command you, brothers, in the name of our Lord Jesus Christ, that you keep away from any brother who is *walking in idleness and not in accord with the tradition* that you received from us" (3:6 my italics). The tradition is no doubt doctrinal, but it is to be lived out accordingly. I will argue below that this tradition can be called "the law of Christ."

Many, many other passages could be cited, but I hope it is clear that the position of this book is only wrongly accused of being antinomian. As we will see, we are under the law of Christ. Also of note is that for Paul, the Mosaic law is not the same thing as the law of God because he says he is not under the Mosaic law but he is not outside the law of God (1 Cor 9:20-21). More about this below.

CHAPTER 6

BUT UNDER THE LAW OF CHRIST

It is clear that we are not under the Mosaic law, but that does not mean we are autonomous individuals. What then, is the law of Christ? Is it the case that New Covenant Theology believes that only what Jesus taught is the standard for believers today? For example, P.G. Nelson describes New Covenant Theology this way in his essay, "Christian Morality: Jesus' Teaching on the Law."[188] I think this is a misrepresentation of New Covenant Theology. There may be some bloggers out there who espouse such a view, but I certainly disagree and have not read anyone who teaches this. While the law of Christ certainly includes the teaching of Jesus, it is more complex than simply what Jesus taught.

The law of Christ is difficult to define due to the fact that there is limited biblical data. The phrase *law of Christ* is only used one time in the Greek New Testament in Galatians 6:2. First Corinthians 9:21 uses the phrase "in-lawed to Christ" (*ennomos Christou*), though most English translations render this phrase as "law of Christ." Since Paul does not explain what this phrase means, it is likely that his congregations were well aware of this phrase and

---

[188] P.G Nelson, "Christian Morality: Jesus' Teaching on the Law," *Themelios* 32, no. 1 (October 2006): 4.

its meaning.[189] With such little exegetical data, we proceed with a theological proposal.

First, it must be emphasized that believers fulfill the law of Christ by the empowering presence of the Holy Spirit (cf. Ezek 36:26-27).[190] Second, and as mentioned above, and worth mentioning again and again, the obedience of believers *flows from* a right standing with God. New Testament scholar Richard Longenecker defines the law of Christ as the "prescriptive principles stemming from the heart of the gospel (usually embodied in the example and teachings of Jesus), which are meant to be applied to specific situations by the direction and enablement of the Holy Spirit, being always motivated and conditioned by love."[191] I think this is a suitable definition. I would only add that the teaching of the Apostles, which for us is the New Testament, is also included in the law of Christ. The law of Christ is the demand of God on new covenant Christians who are no longer bound to the Mosaic law.[192] The law of Christ is the law of God for those who live on this side of the resurrection, the new covenant counterpart to the Mosaic law. God has an eternal moral will; for the old covenant Jew, this was expressed in the Mosaic law. For the new covenant Christian, this moral will is expressed in the law of Christ. However, it is important to note that the two are dislike in many ways. For example, as

[189] Graham Stanton, "The Law of Christ: A Neglected Theological Gem?," in *Reading Texts, Seeking Wisdom*, ed. David F. Ford and Graham Stanton (London: SCM Press, 2003), 173.

[190] Adeyemi, "The Law of Christ," 449.

[191] Longenecker, *Galatians*, 275-76.

[192] Moo, "The Law of Moses or the Law of Christ," 215.

Douglas Moo writes, "Christian behavior ...is now guided directly by 'the law of Christ.' This 'law' does not consist of legal prescriptions and ordinances, but of the teaching and example of Jesus and the apostles, the central demand of love, and the guiding influence of the indwelling Holy Spirit."[193] The law of Christ is not an exhaustive list of rules but principles centered on love, guided by the Spirit, and drawn from the example and teachings of Christ and his apostles, and ultimately drawn from the entire canon viewed through the lens of Jesus Christ.[194] So as we will see, the law of Christ contains specific commandments, but believers are also to be led by the Spirit (Gal 5:16, 18, 25) and be transformed by the renewal of our minds (Rom 12:2).[195]

I want to propose the following five points regarding the law of Christ:

1. The law of Christ is the law of love.
2. The law of Christ is Christ's example.
3. The law of Christ is the teaching of Christ.
4. The law of Christ is the teaching of Christ's apostles.
5. The law of Christ is the whole canon interpreted in light of Christ.

---

[193] Moo, "The Law of Christ as the Fulfillment of the Law of Moses," 343.

[194] Ibid., 357, 361; Longenecker, *Paul: Apostle of Liberty*, 191.

[195] Ibid., 370; Thielman, "Law and Liberty in the Ethics of Paul," 72.

CHAPTER 7

THE LAW OF CHRIST IS
THE LAW OF LOVE

In his Galatians commentary, Martin Luther writes, "The law of Christ is the law of love."[196] Love is absolutely central to the law of Christ. It seems that our circles do not emphasize the centrality of love as the Bible emphasizes the centrality of love. Love is not simply a fuzzy feeling of affection towards another, but self-sacrificially giving of self for the good of others and the glory of God.[197] Love is a verb. God is love (1 John 4:8). He is the self-giving God who calls his people to be self-giving lovers.[198] This is why so many of us are discontent with life. We are living for self rather than for God and for others which is not what we were created for. Christ died for us so that we would no longer live for ourselves (2 Cor 5:15). As Pastor Paul Tripp writes, "To live for yourself is to rob yourself of your own humanity.[199] Read afresh Paul's words in 1 Corinthians 13:

> If I speak in the tongues of men and of angels, but have not *love*, I am a noisy gong or a clanging cymbal. And if I have

---

[196] Martin Luther, *Galatians* (Wheaton, IL: Crossway Books, 1998), 290.

[197] Fee, *God's Empowering Presence*, 446-47; Hill, *The How and Why of Love*, 78, 80, 84, 97.

[198] Keller, *Reason for God*, 215-16.

[199] Paul David Tripp, *A Quest for More* (Greensboro, NC: New Growth Press, 2007), 100.

prophetic powers, and understand all mysteries and all knowledge, and if I have all faith, so as to remove mountains, but have not *love*, I am nothing. If I give away all I have, and if I deliver up my body to be burned, but have not *love*, I gain nothing. *Love* is patient and kind; *love* does not envy or boast; *it* is not arrogant or rude. *It* does not insist on its own way; *it* is not irritable or resentful; *it* does not rejoice at wrongdoing, but rejoices with the truth. *Love* bears all things, believes all things, hopes all things, endures all things. *Love* never ends. As for prophecies, they will pass away; as for tongues, they will cease; as for knowledge, it will pass away. For we know in part and we prophesy in part, but when the perfect comes, the partial will pass away. When I was a child, I spoke like a child, I thought like a child, I reasoned like a child. When I became a man, I gave up childish ways. For now we see in a mirror dimly, but then face to face. Now I know in part; then I shall know fully, even as I have been fully known. So now faith, hope, and *love* abide, these three; but the greatest of these is *love*. (my italics)

In Matthew 22:34-40 Jesus is asked which is the great commandment in the Law. He replies, "You shall love the Lord your God with all your heart and with all your soul and with all your mind. This is the great and first commandment. And a second is like it: You shall love your neighbor as yourself. On these two commandments depend all the Law and the Prophets." Jesus, in Matthew 22:39, quotes Leviticus 19:18b (you shall love your neighbor as yourself), where the neighbor was the fellow Israelite but we know that in the new covenant, our neighbor is anyone in need of help (Luke 10:25-37). We are called to do good to *all*, but especially to those who are of the household of faith (Gal 6:10).

Vertical love and horizontal love are inextricably bound together. Away with the talk of a personal relationship with Jesus that is disconnected to other believers. "Divine love issues in interpersonal love."[200] "*Everything* is done *allēlōn.*"[201] One cannot claim to love Christ without love for the body of Christ. There is an intense unity between Christ and his people. So when Saul was persecuting Christians, Jesus says, "Saul, Saul, why are you persectuting me?" (Acts 9:4, cf. Matt 25:40).[202] John says that if a person claims to love God, yet hates his brother or sister, he is a liar (1 John 4:20). "And this commandment we have from him: whoever loves God must also love his brother" (1 John 4:21).

As mentioned, the phrase *law of Christ* only occurs once in the Bible: Galatians 6:2. Preceding this verse, Paul wrote, "For you were called to freedom, brothers. Only do not use your freedom as an opportunity for the flesh, but through love serve one another. For the whole law is fulfilled in one word: You shall love your neighbor as yourself" (Gal 5:13-14). Amazingly, Paul says that true freedom comes by becoming slaves (*douleuete*) of one another through love![203] The gospel frees us to lovingly serve our brothers and sisters. Then Paul says that the whole law is fulfilled in one

---

[200] Craig L. Blomberg, *Matthew. The New American Commentary,* (Nashville: Broadman Press, 1992), 335.

[201] Fee, *Paul, the Spirit, and the People of God,* 66.

[202] Longenecker, *Paul: Apostle of Liberty,* 204.

[203] Gordon Fee writes, "Freedom from the enslavement of Torah paradoxically means to take on a new form of 'slavery' – that of loving servant hood to one another," *God's Empowering Presence,* 426.

word, citing Leviticus 19:18: You shall love your neighbor as yourself. The one who loves his neighbor has fulfilled what the law demands, and has thus fulfilled the law of Christ (Gal 6:2). Paul's teaching in Romans 13:8-10 is very similar:

> Owe no one anything, except to love each other, for the one who loves another has fulfilled the law. The commandments, "You shall not commit adultery, You shall not murder, You shall not steal, You shall not covet," and any other commandment, are summed up in this word: "You shall love your neighbor as yourself." Love does no wrong to a neighbor; therefore love is the fulfilling of the law.

Love is not at odds with commandments.[204] The commandments not to commit adultery, murder, steal, and covet are simply other ways of saying love your neighbor. James 2:8 says, "If you really fulfill the royal law according to the Scripture, 'You shall love your neighbor as yourself,' you are doing well."

Love is central to the law of Christ.[205] Christians are called to seek the good of our neighbor, not our self (1 Cor 10:24). Above all, we are to put on love, which binds everything together in perfect harmony (Col 3:14). Paul tells Timothy, "The aim of our charge is love that issues from a pure heart and a good conscience and a sincere faith" (1 Tim 1:5). We are to "love one another with brotherly affection" (Rom 12:10). Paul prays that the Lord would make us increase and abound in love for one

---

[204] Horton, Introducing Covenant Theology, 84.

[205] Moo, "The Law of Christ as the Fulfillment of the Law of Moses," 368.

another and for all (1 Thess 3:12). Everything we do is to be done in love (1 Cor 16:24). Peter writes, "Having purified your souls by your obedience to the truth for a sincere brotherly love, love one another earnestly from a pure heart" (1 Pet 1:22). All we do is for the glory of God (1 Cor 10:31), but the immediate context of this verse is all about the other: giving no offense to Jews or Greeks or the church, trying to please everyone in everything we do, not seeking my own advantage but that of many (1 Cor 10:32-33).

John also emphasizes the centrality of love. Whoever loves his brother abides in the light (1 John 2:10). The one who does not love his brother is not a child of God, but of the devil (1 John 3:10). "For this is the message that you have heard from the beginning, that we should love one another" (1 John 3:11, cf. 2 John 5-6). "We know that we have passed out of death into life, because we love the brothers. Whoever does not love abides in death" (1 John 3:14). "By this we know love, that he laid down his life for us, and we ought to lay down our lives for the brothers" (1 John 3:16). "And this is his commandment, that we believe in the name of his Son Jesus Christ and love one another, just as he has commanded us" (1 John 3:23).

First Thessalonians 4:7-9 is a very informative passage for the centrality of love in the new covenant law of Christ: "For God has not called us for impurity, but in holiness. Therefore whoever disregards this, disregards not man but God, who gives his Holy Spirit to you. Now concerning brotherly love, you have no need for anyone to write to you, for you yourselves have been taught by God to love one another." Three key Old Testament new covenant passages are Jeremiah 31, Isaiah 54, and Ezekiel 36, and Paul alludes to all three in this important passage. The Lord had prophesied through the prophet Ezekiel that he would "sprinkle clean water on you, and you shall be clean from all your uncleannesses, and from all your idols I will cleanse you. And I will give you a new heart, and a new spirit I will put within you. And I will remove the heart of stone from your flesh and give you a heart of flesh. And I will put my Spirit within you, and cause you to walk in my statutes and be careful to obey my rules" (Ezek 36:25-27, cf. 11:19).

In the new age the Lord would pour out his Spirit empowering the new Israel to walk in obedience. In chapter thirty-seven, Ezekiel recalled the valley of the dry bones upon whom YHWH would pour out his Spirit and bring life to the dead (37:6, 14). Paul is clearly alluding to this passage in 1 Thessalonians 4:8:[206]

1 Thess 4:8: _kai didonta to pneuma autou to hagion eis hymas_

Ezek 36:27 LXX: _kai to pneuma mou dōsō en hymin_

Ezek 37:14 LXX: _kai dōsō to pneuma mou eis hymas_

1 Thess 4:8: who gives his Holy Spirit to you

Ezek 36:27: And I will put my Spirit within you

Ezek 37:14: And I will put my Spirit within you

---

[206] T.J Deidun, _New Covenant Morality in Paul_ (Rome: Biblical Institute Press, 1981), 18-22, 55-57; Jeffrey A.D Weima, "1-2 Thessalonians," in _Commentary on the New Testament Use of the Old Testament_, ed. G.K. Beale and D.A. Carson (Grand Rapids: Baker Academic, 2007), 878-880.

We have seen above that the New Testament writers
viewed the new covenant as having been inaugurated by
the death and resurrection of Jesus Christ. The Spirit was
poured out at Pentecost (Acts 2). We have God's Spirit and
a new heart.[207] Jesus appeals to Ezekiel 36 in his
conversation with Nicodemus: "unless one is born of water
and the Spirit, he cannot enter the kingdom of God. That
which is born of the flesh is flesh, and that which is born of
the Spirit is spirit" (John 3:5-6).[208] Jesus rebuked him for not
being familiar with this truth, though he was a teacher of
Israel. The new covenant is here, bringing with it the new
birth where we are given the Spirit and a new heart. Being
born from above enables and empowers believers to love
one another. "Beloved, let us love one another, for love is
from God, and whoever loves has *been born of God* and
knows God" (1 John 4:7 my italics).

In the next verse, Paul says, "Now concerning brotherly
love, you have no need for anyone to write to you, for you
yourselves have been taught by God to love one another"
(1 Thess 4:9). Because the Thessalonians have been given
the new covenant promise of the Spirit, they have no need
for instruction (though Paul is writing them in this verse)
because they have been taught by God (*theodidaktoi*) to love
one another. Paul makes up this word "*theodidaktoi*" but he
is surely alluding to at least two passages: Isaiah 54 and
Jeremiah 31, where we find promises that in the new

---

[207] Commenting on 1 Thess 4:8, Gordon Fee writes, "This usage reflects
a Pauline understanding of the gift of the Spirit as the fulfillment of
OT promises that God's own Spirit will come to indwell his
people," *God's Empowering Presence*, 52.

[208] Carson, *John*, 194-95.

covenant age God himself will teach his people.[209] In Jeremiah's great new covenant passage we read, "I will put my law within them, and I will write it on their hearts. And I will be their God, and they shall be my people. And no longer shall each one teach his neighbor and each his brother, saying, 'Know the Lord,' for they shall all know me, from the least of them to the greatest, declares the Lord" (Jer 31:33-34; cf. 2 Cor 3:3). In the new covenant, we are *taught by God*. All will know the Lord. Putting together several texts (Jer 31, Ezek 11, 36, Joel 2) we see that all will know the Lord because all will have the Spirit. John writes, "But the anointing that you received from him abides in you, and you have no need that anyone should teach you" (1 John 2:27). John was clearly aware of the promises of Jeremiah 31 and Ezekiel 36.[210]

Paul also clearly alludes to (or quotes) Isaiah 54:13: "All your children shall be taught by the Lord (*didaktous theou*)."[211] Isaiah is referring to the children of the new covenant (cf. Gal 4:27, John 6:45). Of course this chapter is in the midst of the "gospel of the Old Testament," chapters 40-55, and it follows chapter fifty-three, the magnificent portrait of the suffering servant who will bring it all about. Isaiah 54 paints a picture of the new covenant, in light of the other covenants. Verses one to three contain allusions to the Abrahamic Covenant (Sarah's barrenness, room for Gentiles, offspring possessing the nations), verses 4-8 allude to the Mosaic Covenant (deserted wife, exile,

---

[209] Deidun, *New Covenant Morality in Paul*, 20. Weima, "1-2 Thessalonians," 879.

[210] Ibid.

[211] Ibid.

Babylon), 9-17 alludes to the Noahic covenant. Verse ten speaks of the covenant of peace. This is equivalent to the new covenant and "will be the fulfillment of all previous covenants."[212] Paul sees this time as having arrived. The law is written not on tablets of stone but on our heart (2 Cor 3:3). We are taught by God. Paul goes a step further in defining what we are taught: *to love one another* (1 Thess 4:9)! This is the essence of the law (as we have seen from Matt 22:37-38, Gal 5:14, Rom 13:8-10). Love is at the heart of the law of Christ.

---

[212] Barry G. Webb, *The Message of Isaiah* (Downers Grove, IL: Inter-Varsity Press, 1996), 215. I am indebted to Webb for this whole paragraph.

CHAPTER 8

THE LAW OF CHRIST IS
THE EXAMPLE OF CHRIST

Bound up with love is the example of Christ. After all, it is Christ's giving up of himself on the cross that is the paradigm for love. In John 13, Christ gives his people a *new* commandment: "A new commandment I give to you, that you love one another." We have just seen how important this self-giving love is, but Jesus continues, "just as I have loved you, you also are to love one another. By this all people will know that you are my disciples, if you have love for one another" (John 13:34-35, cf 1 John 2:7-8).[213] Jesus shows us what it means to love one another. Elsewhere John writes, "By this we know love, that he laid down his life for us, and we ought to lay down our lives for the brothers" (1 John 3:16). The love of God was made manifest to us in that God sent his Son so that we might have life (1 John 4:9). "This is love, not that we loved God but that he loved us and sent his Son to be the propitiation for our sins" (1 John 4:10, cf. 4:19). If God has loved us in this way (*houtōs*), we also ought to love one another (1 John 4:11). If we love others, God abides in us and his love is perfected in us (1 John 4:12). Those bound to the Mosaic law did not have this great example of what it means to have self-sacrificial, Calvary-like love. This command is

---

[213] Carson, *John*, 484-85.

new because of the cross of Christ, and as Frank Thielman writes, the new commandment "implies that the old commandment is no longer in force."[214] Jason Meyer writes, "The love command is not new in the sense that no one ever knew about God's command to love others. It is new in the sense that believers should love one another 'as I have loved you'."[215]

We are to imitate Christ in this sense. Many evangelicals have rightly defended penal substitutionary atonement (i.e. Christ paying the penalty for our sins) as the heart of the atonement,[216] but in doing so we are not throwing out the other 'models.' Christ as example is an important motif in Scripture. Paul commands his churches to imitate him as he imitates Christ (1 Cor 11:1, Phil 3:17, Gal 4:12, 1 Thess 1:6). In this sense, the law of Christ is Christ himself![217] So Gordon Fee says of Paul's ethics (which is part of what we

---

[214] Frank Thielman, *The Law and the New Testament: The Question of Continuity* (New York: The Crossroad Publishing Company, 1999), 177.

[215] Meyer, *The End of the Law*, 286.

[216] E.g. see Thomas R. Schreiner's contribution in *The Nature of the Atonement*, ed. James Beilby and Paul R. Eddy (Downers Grove, IL: IVP Academic, 2006).

[217] Fee, *God's Empowering Presence*, 463-64; Seifrid, *Christ, Our Righteousness*, 97. Unlike these scholars though, I am arguing that there are actual commands contained in the law of Christ. That the law of Christ is Christ himself is only part of the law of Christ. The New Testament has more to say. Although Justin Martyr does speak in places of Christ as a law*giver*, he also says that Christ himself is our "everlasting and final law," in *Dialogue with Trypho*, trans. Thomas B. Falls (Washington D.C.: The Catholic University of America Press, 2003), 20.

are dealing with): "God's glory is their *purpose*, the Spirit is their *power*, love is the *principle*, and Christ is the *pattern*."[218]

In Galatians 6:2 we are *commanded* to "bear one another's burdens, and so fulfill the law of Christ." All throughout Galatians we are shown that it is Christ Jesus who is the ultimate burden-bearer in his self-giving love on the cross. He "gave himself for our sins to deliver us from the present evil age" (Gal 1:4). The Son of God loved us and gave himself for us (Gal 2:20). "Christ redeemed us from the curse of the law by becoming a curse for us" (Gal 3:13). He redeemed those under that law so that we might receive adoption as sons (Gal 4:5). Jesus Christ is the paradigm for Christian love.[219]

In Romans 15:1-3, the strong (with regard to food) are called to bear with the weak, and not to please ourselves. Paul is using the same word for *bear* (*bastazō)* here as he did in Galatians 6:2. He continues, "Let each of us please his neighbor for his good, to build him up" (Rom 15:2). But what is important for this section is the reason Paul gives: "For [*gar*] Christ did not please himself" (Rom 15:3a). Again, Christ is the great example of what it means to love our neighbor rather than pleasing ourselves.[220]

It's important to note that when issuing commands to the churches, the New Testament writers rarely appeal to the Mosaic law, but often appeal to Christ and his gospel.

---

[218] Ibid., 463.

[219] Richard B. Hays, "Christology and Ethics in Galatians: The Law of Christ," *The Catholic Biblical Quarterly* 49, no. 1 (January 1987): 273. Hays says the law of Christ is the paradigmatic self-giving of Jesus Christ (275). I agree, but again, the New Testament has more to say.

[220] Ibid., 287. See Moo, *Romans*, 866.

Paul's ethic is a gospel-driven ethic. Our evangel informs our ethic. Christian husbands should love their wives *as Christ loved the church* (Eph 5:25). Christians should love one another *as Christ has loved us* (John 13:34). When Paul wants to encourage the Corinthians to give generously, he writes, "For you know the grace of our Lord Jesus Christ, that though he was rich, yet for your sake he became poor, so that you by his poverty might become rich" (2 Cor 8:9). Christians should forgive one another *as God in Christ forgave us* (Eph 4:32, Col 3:13). We are to walk in love *as Christ loved us and gave himself up for us* (Eph 5:2).[221]

We are to do nothing out of selfish ambition or conceit, but "…in humility count others more significant than yourselves. Let each of you look not only to his own interests, but also to the interests of others. Have this mind among yourselves, which is yours in Christ Jesus, who though he was in the form of God, did not count equality with God a thing to be grasped, but made himself nothing, taking the form of a servant, being born in the likeness of men. And being found in human form, he humbled himself by becoming obedient to the point of death, even death on a cross" (Phil 2:3-8). Children are to obey their parents *in the Lord* (Eph 6:1). When we suffer for doing good we need to know that this is what we have been called to …because Christ also suffered for you, leaving you an example, so that you might follow in his steps" (1 Pet 2:21). Set your minds on things above and not on earthly things because (*gar*) "…you have died, and your life is hidden with Christ

---

[221] See Fred G. Zaspel's excellent article, "The Apostolic Model for Christian Ministry: An Analysis of 1 Corinthians 2:1-5," *Reformation & Revival* 7, no. 1 (Winter 1998): 20-34.

in God" (Col 3:2-3). In 1 Corinthians 6:12-20 Paul could have easily appealed to the seventh commandment of the Decalogue but that is not what he does. He says, "Do you not know that your bodies are members of Christ? Shall I then take the members of Christ and make them members of a prostitute? Never!" (1 Cor 6:15). In Romans 6:1-14 we are taught that we are not to continue in sin because we have died with and been raised with Christ. Paul's call to obedience is ever and always *gospel-driven*.

CHAPTER 9

THE LAW OF CHRIST IS
THE TEACHING OF CHRIST

This is a rather obvious point. Most would agree that the law of Christ includes his teaching. For the New Testament writers, the law of Christ is not only his example and person, but also his teaching.[222] He is our great prophet.

Christ Our Prophet

The Old Testament anticipated an eschatological prophet to come. Deuteronomy 18:15-18 says, "The LORD your God will raise up for you a prophet like me from among you, from your brothers—it is to him you shall listen—just as you desired of the LORD your God at Horeb on the day of the assembly, when you said, 'Let me not hear again the voice of the LORD my God or see this great fire any more, lest I die.' And the LORD said to me, 'They are right in what they have spoken. I will raise up for them a prophet like you from among their brothers. And I will put my words in his mouth, and he shall speak to them all that I command him." Moses is here referring to a sequence of prophets and one final unique prophet who will be like Moses.[223] YHWH said of Moses: "If there is a prophet

---

[222] Longenecker, *Paul: Apostle of Liberty*, 191, 194.

[223] Contra Daniel I. Block who argues that this passage should only be interpreted collectively. Commenting on the NT usage of Deuteronomy 18, he writes, "Even if Peter and/or Stephen viewed

among you, I the LORD make myself known to him in a vision; I speak with him in a dream. Not so with my servant Moses. He is faithful in all my house. With him I speak mouth to mouth, clearly, and not in riddles, and he beholds the form of the Lord" (Numb 12:6b-8a). Moses was the inaugurator of the Old Covenant and the pinnacle of the prophetic institution. Deuteronomy 34:9-12 sets out an eschatological expectation for the coming Moses-like prophet: "And there has not arisen a prophet since in Israel like Moses, whom the LORD knew face to face, none like him for all the signs and the wonders that the LORD sent him do to in the land of Egypt" (v.10-11a).

The prophetic institution reached its culmination in Christ.[224] The New Testament presents Jesus as the one to whom the prophets pointed.[225] Luke 24:27 says, "Beginning with Moses and all the Prophets, he interpreted to them in all the Scriptures the things concerning himself" (cf. Luke

---

Jesus as a messianic prophet 'like Moses,' are we thereby authorized to read their use of Deut. 18:15 back into the original context?" in "My Servant David: Ancient Israel's Vision of the Messiah," in Israel's Messiah in the Bible and The Dead Sea Scrolls, ed. Hess, Richard S. and M. Daniel Carroll R (Grand Rapids: Baker Academic, 2003), 29-32. The implied answer for Block is "no." If one's exegesis of the OT does not align with the apostolic exegesis of the OT, one probably ought to humbly return to the drawing board.

[224] Graeme Goldsworthy, *Preaching the Whole Bible as Christian Scripture* (Grand Rapids: Eerdmans, 2000), 42; Samuel J. Mikolaski, "The Mediatorial Offices of Christ: Prophet, Priest, King," in *Basic Christian Doctrines*, ed. Henry, Carl F.H (New York: Holt, Rinehart and Winston, 1962), 148.

[225] N.T Wright, *The Last Word: Scripture and the Authority of God-Getting Beyond the Bible Wars* (New York: HarperOne, 2005), 42-44.

24:44-47, 1 Pet 1:10-12). Jesus claimed that Moses wrote about *him* (John 5:46). Jesus is the chief and last prophet typified in the Old Testament.[226] This is why the priests and Levites respond in the way they do, and ask, "What then? Are you Elijah? He said, 'I am not.' Are you the prophet?" (Jn 1:21). After feeding the five thousand, the people said, "This is indeed the Prophet who is to come into the World" (Jn 6:14, cf. 1:25, 45, 7:40). When Jesus, Peter, John, James, Moses, and Elijah are on the mountain, "a voice came out of the cloud, saying 'This is my Son, my Chosen One; listen to him' (*autou akouete*)" (Lk 9:35)! Note the allusion to Deuteronomy 18 where YHWH said the people *would listen* to the prophet to come (*autou akousesthe* LXX). The reader is not left to allusions though because Acts 3:22 and 7:37 applies the Deuteronomy passage to Jesus as the eschatological prophet. Commenting on Acts 3:22, David Peterson writes, "Peter envisages Jesus as the eschatological prophet because he brings the ultimate revelation of God's will and leads God's people to final salvation. Jesus functions for Israel now as Moses did at the time of the exodus."[227]

---

[226] Robert Letham, *The Work of Christ* (Downers Grove: InterVarsity Press, 1993), 94-95.

[227] Peterson, *The Acts of the Apostles*, 183-84, cf. 257. Commenting on these passages, Luther writes, "For since God here promises another Moses whom they are to hear, it follows of necessity that this other one would teach something different from Moses; and Moses gives up his power and yields to him, so that men will listen to him. This [coming] prophet cannot, then, teach the law, for Moses has done that to perfection; for the law's sake there would be no need to raise up another prophet. Therefore this word was surely spoken

This prophet, however, is much greater than any Old Testament prophet.[228] Scripture presents Jesus as greater than Moses. In Matthew, Jesus is the new Moses who goes up on the mount to give the new covenant law (Matt 5-7). While Moses was a faithful *servant in* all God's house, Jesus is the faithful *Son over* God's house (Heb 3:1-6). Hebrews 1:1-2a says, "Long ago, at many times and in many ways, God spoke to our fathers by the prophets, but in these last days he has spoken to us by his Son" (*en huiō*). Theologian Robert Letham writes, "In the mind of the author of Hebrews Jesus Christ, God's Son, is a prophet, the greatest prophet and the final definitive prophet, since he is superior to prophets, angels, Moses and all other possible competitors."[229]

All throughout Jesus' ministry, he is referred to as a prophet (Matt 13:57, Mark 8:28, Matt 21:46, Luke 7:16, Mark 14:65).[230] He spoke as one with authority (Matt 7:29), and it was on his own authority, unlike the prophets who only spoke with authority when under the influence of the Spirit. Hence, Peter tells Jesus that he has the words of life (John 6:68). "Jesus' words are the foundation of the church

---

concerning Christ and the teaching of grace," "Preface to the Old Testament," in *Martin Luther's Basic Theological Writings,* 129.

[228] John Wenham, *Christ and the Bible* (Grand Rapids: Baker Books, 1994), 59.

[229] Letham, *Work of Christ,* 95

[230] See N.T. Wright, *Jesus and the Victory of God* (Minneapolis: Fortress Press, 1996), 147-97 for more Scriptural evidence and exposition of Jesus as a prophet.

and of the Christian life. Without them we are lost."[231] In
the antitheses of Matthew 5:21-48, Jesus says "You have
heard that it was said...But I say to you." Jesus is the
sovereign lawgiver.[232] His teaching is authoritative because
he speaks just as the Father taught him (John 8:28, cf. 5:24-
27).

The Teaching of Jesus in the Teaching of the Apostles

The law of Christ obviously includes the "red letters" of
our prophet and although the rest of the New Testament
authors do not often directly quote the teaching of Jesus,
they allude to it all the time. Richard Longenecker shows
how Paul is clearly dependent upon the teaching of
Jesus.[233] He shows the overlap between Paul and Jesus in
Romans twelve to fourteen:

> **Romans 12:14** "Bless those who persecute you; bless and
> do not curse them." (Cf. Matt 5:44)

> **Romans 12:17** "Repay no one evil for evil, but give thought
> to do what is honorable in the sight of all." (cf. Matt 5:39)

> **Romans 12:21** "Do not be overcome by evil, but overcome
> evil with good." (Cf. Jesus teaching on nonresistance).

> **Romans 13:7** "Pay to all what is owed to them: taxes to
> whom taxes are owed, revenue to whom revenue is owed,
> respect to whom respect is owed, honor to whom honor is
> owed." (Cf. Matt 22:15-22; Mark 12:13-17; Luke 20:20-26).

---

[231] John M. Frame, *Salvation Belongs to the Lord* (Phillipsburg, NJ: P&R
Publishing, 2006), 54.

[232] Letham, Work of Christ, 93.

[233] See Longenecker, *Paul: Apostle of Liberty*, 189-90. See also C.H Dodd,
More New Testament Studies (Grand Rapids: Eerdmans, 1968), 144-45.

Romans 13:8-10 "Owe no one anything, except to love each other, for the one who loves another has fulfilled the law. For the commandments, 'You shall not commit adultery, You shall not murder, You shall not steal, You shall not covet,' and any other commandment, are summed up in this word: 'You shall love your neighbor as yourself.' Love does no wrong to a neighbor; therefore love is the fulfilling of the law." (Cf. Matt 22:34-40; Mark 12:28-34; Luke 10:25-28).

Romans 14:10 "Why do you pass judgment on your brother? Or you, why do you despise your brother? For we will all stand before the judgment seat of God." (Cf. Matt 7:1; Luke 6:37).

Romans 14:13 "Therefore let us not pass judgment on one another any longer, but rather decide never to put a stumbling block or hindrance in the way of a brother." (Cf. Matt 18:7; Mark 9:42 Luke 17:1-2).

Romans 14:14 "I know and am persuaded in the Lord Jesus that nothing is unclean in itself, but it is unclean for anyone who thinks it unclean." (Cf. Matt 15:11; Mark 7:15).

Romans 14:17 "For the kingdom of God is not a matter of eating and drinking but of righteousness and peace and joy in the Holy Spirit." (Cf. Jesus' teaching on the kingdom of God in the synoptics).

Even our big text, Galatians 6:1-2, is dependent on the teaching of Jesus.[234] When Paul tells the Galatians to restore a person caught in transgression in a spirit of gentleness (Gal 6:1), he surely has Jesus' teaching on restoring sinning brothers and sisters in Matthew 18:15-20 in abbreviated form. Galatians 6:2 alludes to Matthew 23:4. Unlike the

---

[234] Dodd, *More New Testament Studies*, 146; A. Andrew Das, *Paul and the Jews* (Peabody, MA: Hendrickson, 2003), 170.

scribes and Pharisees, who "tie up heavy [barēa] burdens, hard to bear, and lay them on people's shoulders, but they themselves are not willing to move them with their finger" (Matt 23:4), the Israel of God (Gal 6:16) is called to bear one another's burdens (barē), and so fulfill the law of Christ (Gal 6:2).

Slaves of Christ

Another name for a Christian is a slave[235] of Christ (Rom 1:1, Gal 1:10, Eph 6:5-6, Col 4:12, Tit 1:1, 1 Cor 7:22, Jam 1:1, 2 Pet 1:1, Jude 1, Rev 1:1).[236] The risen Christ is our *master*.[237] Jesus is our authority.[238] We are owned by him. There is a

---

[235] The ESV, like most English translations, softens the language by translating *doulos* as "servant." *BDAG* notes that "servant" as a translation is largely confined to Biblical translation and early American times, but in normal usage at the present time the two words are carefully distinguished. Murray Harris writes, "A servant gives service to someone, but a slave belongs to someone," Murray J. Harris, *Slave of Christ: A New Testament Metaphor for Total Devotion to Christ* (Downers Grove, IL: Inter-Varsity Press, 1999), 18.

[236] And as we have seen above, to be a slave of Christ is to be a slave to one another (Gal 5:13-14). Murray Harris writes, "The term *doulos* expresses both a vertical and a horizontal relationship of the Christian, who is both the willing vassal of the heavenly Master and the submissive servant of fellow-believers. The term epitomizes the Christian's dual obligation: unquestioning devotion to Christ and to his people. But the vertical relationship is prior and the horizontal secondary. Christians are devoted to one another as a direct result of being devoted to Christ. When they serve each other, they are demonstrating and expressing their slavery to the Lord Christ" *Slave of Christ*, 104-05.

[237] Tom Wells and Fred Zaspel, *New Covenant Theology* (Frederick, MD: New Covenant Media, 2002), 14-15.

[238] See Tom Wells, *The Priority of Jesus Christ* (Frederick, MD: New Covenant Media, 2005).

sense in which all people are owned by Christ since all things were made through him (John 1:3, 1 Cor 8:6, Col 1:16, Heb 1:2), but believers are "twice-owned," created and redeemed by Jesus Christ (1 Cor 6:20). We are to listen to *him* (Matt 17:5). Jesus is our authority, for *all* authority has been given to him (Matt 28:18).[239] Our commission is to go and teach all to observe all that *Jesus commanded*. The 1646 London Confession of Faith rightly reflects this when it says that the believer is to "presseth after a heavenly and evangelical obedience to all the commands, which Christ as head and king in his new covenant hath prescribed to them."[240] Paul sent Timothy to the Corinthians to remind them of his ways in Christ, as he taught everywhere in every church (1 Cor 4:17). This word *ways* (*hodous*) implies both lifestyle and doctrine, which are intimately bound together in the Bible.[241]

There has been a shift in authority from the old covenant law to the law of Christ.[242] The law was given through

---

[239] I. Howard Marshall writes, "The law is taken up into a new expression of the will of God as taught by Jesus, and at the end of the Gospel the disciples are to teach people 'to obey everything that I have commanded you' – with no mention of law," *New Testament Theology* (Downers Grove, IL: InterVarsity Press, 2004), 119.

[240] *The First London Confession of Faith* (Belton, TX: Sovereign Grace Ministries, 2004), 11-12.

[241] Gordon D. Fee, *The First Epistle to the Corinthians.* The New International Commentary on the New Testament (Grand Rapids: Eerdmans, 1987), 189.

[242] Douglas Moo writes, "What emerges from Jesus' teaching is a shift of focus from the law to Jesus himself as the criterion for what it means to be obedient to God," "The Law of Christ as the Fulfillment of the Law of Moses," 357.

Moses but grace and truth came through Jesus Christ (John 1:17). As Thomas Schreiner notes, "John does not concentrate on commands that stem from the OT law. Instead as we would expect from John 1:17, the emphasis lies upon what Jesus instructs his disciples to do. He speaks of 'my commandments' (14:15, 21; 15:10) and 'my commandment' (15:12), and what "I command you' (15:14, 17), and the 'new commandment' that 'I give to you' (13:34). The law has reached its fulfillment in Christ, and his commands are authoritative for believers."[243]

---

[243] Schreiner, *40 Questions*, 226.

CHAPTER 10

THE LAW OF CHRIST IS THE TEACHING OF CHRIST'S APOSTLES

Christ and His Apostles

The relation of Christ and His apostles is a tight one; much tighter than many would like. Jesus appointed apostles to continue his prophetic ministry.[244] He set apart twelve men for this task (Matt 10:1, Mark 3:13-19) and commissioned them as representatives and ambassadors (Acts 10:41).[245] The Lord gave them their authority. This was similar to the *shaliach* in Judaism. In the Jewish legal system, the *shaliach* was given legal power to represent another person, and "so unique was his relationship to the one he represented that the *shaliach* was regarded as that

---

[244] Robert Letham notes three prominent characteristics of the apostles: a) They received a definite appointment from Christ himself. b) They were associated with the ministry of Jesus from the beginning (Paul being a major exception but he was aware of this). c) They functioned as witnesses of Christ's resurrection, in *Work of Christ*, 97.

[245] Ibid., 95. Herman Ridderbos writes, "For the *communication* and *transmission* of what was seen and heard in the fullness of time, Christ established a *formal authority structure to be the source and standard for all future preaching of the gospel*," in *Redemptive History and the New Testament Scriptures* (Grand Rapids: Baker Book House, 1963), 13.

person himself."[246] So Jesus can say to them, "The one who hears you hears me, and the one who rejects you rejects me, and the one who rejects me rejects him who sent me" (Luke 10:16) (cf. Matt 10:40, Mark 9:37, John 13:20, 17:8). John 14-16 are crucial chapters in this regard. Jesus tells his disciples:

> These things I have spoken to you while I am still with you. But the Helper, the Holy Spirit, whom the Father will send in my name, he will teach you all things and bring to your remembrance all that I have said to you (14:25-26)…But when the Helper comes, whom I will send to you from the Father, the Spirit of truth, who proceeds from the Father, he will bear witness about me. And you also will bear witness, because you have been with me from the beginning (15:26-27)…When the Spirit of truth comes, he will guide you into all the truth, for he will not speak on his own authority, but whatever he hears he will speak, and he will declare to you the things that are to come (16:13).

Jesus is clear here, that he would ascend and then send the Spirit to guide the apostles.[247] Robert Letham writes, "Through this appointment the apostles received the

---

[246] Ridderbos, *Redemptive History and the New Testament Scriptures*, 14; cf. Wenham, *Christ and the Bible,* 119; Letham, *Work of Christ,* 95.

[247] D.A Carson notes, "John's purpose in including this theme and this verse [John 14:25-26] is not to explain how readers at the end of the first century may be taught by the Spirit, but to explain to readers at the end of the first century how the first witnesses, the first disciples, came to an accurate and full understanding of the truth of Jesus Christ. The Spirit's ministry in this respect was not to bring qualitatively new revelation, but to complete, to fill out, the revelation brought by Jesus himself," in *The Gospel According to John* (Grand Rapids: Eerdmans, 1991), 505.

authority of Christ and became his ambassadors, representing him in the church and in the world. Hence forth, their teaching was to be Christ's own teaching, no less."[248]

Therefore, the authority of the apostles, now found in the New Testament, is bound up with the authority of the risen Christ himself. Their teaching is his teaching. The prophets and apostles are the foundation of the church (Eph 2:20). The Apostle Paul can say, "Assuming that you have heard of the stewardship of God's grace that was given to me for you, how the mystery was made known to me by revelation...the mystery of Christ, which was not made known to the sons of men in other generations as it has now been revealed to his holy apostles and prophets by the Spirit" (Eph 3:2-5).[249] Paul did not receive his gospel from people, but received it through a revelation of Jesus Christ (Gal 1:11-12). The Thessalonians received the word of God from the apostles "not as the word of men but as what it really is, the word of God" (1 Thess 2:13b, cf. 1 Cor 2:12-13). In his high priestly prayer, Jesus prays, "I do not ask for these only, but also for those who will believe in me through their word" (John 17:20). Jesus and the apostolic word are inextricably bound together. This is why the early

---

[248] Letham, *Work of Christ*, 96-97.

[249] On the supposed contradiction between Paul and Jesus, see David Wenham, *Paul: Follower of Jesus or Founder of Christianity* (Grand Rapids: Eerdmans, 1995); idem, *Paul and Jesus: The True Story* (Grand Rapids: Eerdmans, 2002); J. Gresham Machen, *The Origin of Paul's Religion* (Grand Rapids: Eerdmans, 1925); Herman Ridderbos, *Paul and Jesus* (Philadelphia: The Presbyterian and Reformed Publishing Company, 1958); N.T. Wright, *What Saint Paul Really Said.*

church was devoted to the *apostle's* teaching (Acts 2:42). Also, Paul can tell the Ephesians, whom Jesus *never visited*, that Jesus "came and preached peace to you" (Eph 2:17). First John 4:6b says, "Whoever knows God listens to us; whoever is not from God does not listen to us." The consequence of this teaching is that those who want to be faithful to Christ *must* be faithful to the New Testament Scriptures (which presuppose the authority of the Hebrew Scriptures). As Letham says, "There can be no dichotomy between Jesus and the apostles. We are offered Christ clothed with the apostolic gospel. That is the way God intended and executed it. No other option is given us."[250] So the law of Christ necessarily includes the teachings of Jesus and the teaching of the Apostles, which for us is the New Testament.[251]

Although James uses different terminology, he agrees with the rest of the New Testament witness. The perfect law, the law of liberty, and the royal law (Ja 1:25, 2:8, 2:12) are referring to the same concept as the law of Christ.[252] James probably uses the perfect to refer to the law in its eschatological fullness. According to Douglas Moo, James uses "royal" "to connote the law pertaining to the kingdom of God. As with the phrase 'the perfect law that gives freedom' in 1:25, then, 'royal law' might be James's way of

---

[250] Letham, *Work of Christ*, 99; see also Reisinger, *But I Say Unto You*, 25.

[251] Tom Wells, *The Priority of Jesus Christ* (Frederick, MD: New Covenant Media, 2005), 132; Wells and Zaspel, *New Covenant Theology*, 40.

[252] Long, *Biblical Law and Ethics*, 91; Wayne G. Strickland, "The Inauguration of the Law of Christ with the Gospel of Christ," in *Five Views on Law and Gospel*, 277; Schreiner, *New Testament Theology*, 663-65.

referring to the sum total of demands that God, through Jesus, imposes on believers."[253] It is unlikely that these phrases refer to the Mosaic law.[254] If it did, surely mention would be made of circumcision, the Sabbath, and food laws.[255] This "law of liberty" in verse twenty-five must be interpreted in light of the "word" of verses twenty-two and twenty-three, which itself is closely related to "the word of truth that brought us forth" (i.e. regenerated us – Ja 1:18). In 1:21, we are commanded to receive the implanted word, which is able to save your souls.[256] This phrase "implanted word" points back to the new covenant promises of Jeremiah 31 and Ezekiel 36 (hence law *of liberty*).[257] The royal law is the law of King Jesus, who through the power of the promised Spirit gives freedom.

Believers are bound to every imperative in the New Testament. As Jonathan Edwards puts it, the New Testament is "the charter and municipal law of the christian church."[258] The New Testament is the "church's foundation documents."[259]

---

[253] Douglas J. Moo, *The Letter of James*. The Pillar New Testament Commentary (Grand Rapids: Eerdmans, 2000), 112.

[254] Moo suggests that "James's 'law' does not refer to the law of Moses as such, but to the law of Moses as interpreted and supplemented by Christ," Ibid., 94.

[255] Schreiner, *40 Questions*, 236.

[256] Moo, *The Letter of James*, 94.

[257] Ibid; Schreiner, *New Testament Theology*, 663; idem, *40 Questions*, 237.

[258] Here is the full quotation: "There is perhaps no part of divinity attended with so much intricacy, and wherein orthodox divines do so much differ, as the stating of the precise agreement and difference between the two dispensations of Moses and of Christ. And probably the reason why God has left it so intricate, is because

our understanding the ancient dispensation, and God's design in it, is not of so great importance, nor does it so nearly concern us. Since God uses great plainness of speech in the New Testament, which is as it were the charter and municipal law of the christian church, what need we run back to the ceremonial and typical institutions of an antiquated dispensation, wherein God's declared design was, to deliver divine things in comparative obscurity, hid under a veil, and involved in clouds?" "An Humble Inquiry," 465.

[259] Reisinger, Tablets of Stone, 111.

CHAPTER 11

THE LAW OF CHRIST IS
THE WHOLE CANON
INTERPRETED IN
LIGHT OF CHRIST

Sometimes New Covenant Theology is charged with being Marcionite, i.e. neglecting the Hebrew Scriptures. There may indeed be some who claim the label who do this very thing, but they are wrong to do so. Ultimately, the new covenant believer is bound to the entire canon of Scripture, with this very important qualification: *interpreted in light of Christ.*[260] All of it is God's Word for us. *All*

---

[260] John Reisinger writes, "'We believe the Ten Commandments, as *interpreted and applied by our Lord in his teaching and in the Holy Spirit-inspired New Covenant Scriptures,* are a vital part of our rule of life. The entire Bible, all sixty-six books, as it is interpreted through the lens of the New Covenant Scriptures, is our rule of life.' This is the essence of New Covenant Theology's hermeneutic concerning law," *But I Say Unto You,* 16, 157-58; idem, *Tablets of Stone,* 35, 109, 113, 127. Douglas J. Moo, "Law," in *Dictionary of Jesus and the Gospels,* ed. Joel B. Green, Scot McKnight, and I. Howard Marshall (Downers Grove, IL: InterVarstity Press, 1992), 461; idem, "The Law of Moses or the Law of Christ," 206, 217; idem, "The Law of Christ as the Fulfillment of the Law of Moses," 353; idem, "Jesus and the Authority of the Mosaic Law," 28, 30; David Peterson, *Possessed by God* (Downers Grove, IL: InterVarsity Press,1995), 146; D.A. Carson, *Matthew,* Vol. 1. in *The Expositors Bible Commentary,* ed. Frank E. Gaebelein (Grand Rapids, MI: Zondervan, 1995), 144, 146;

Scripture (obviously referring to the Old Testament) is God-breathed and profitable for teaching, for reproof, for correction, and for training in righteousness, that the man of God may be competent, equipped for every good work (cf. 2 Tim 3:16, 17).[261] Whatever was written in former days was written for our instruction (Rom 15:4). The Old Testament events happened to them as an example and were "written down for our instruction, on whom the end of the ages has come" (1 Cor 10:11b). Believers in Jesus are the children of Abraham (Gal 3:7, 29, 6:16, Phil 3:3) and the Old Testament is _our_ book but we must approach it _as Christians._. As Graham Cole writes, "Christian students of the Old Testament _must pass by the cross of Jesus Christ on their return to the Old Testament._"[262]

Matthew 5:17-48

We gain this perspective from Jesus teaching in Matthew chapter five.[263] There Jesus famously says:

> Do not think that I have come to abolish the Law or the Prophets; I have not come to abolish them but to fulfill them. For truly, I say to you, until heaven and earth pass away, not an iota, not a dot, will pass from the Law until all is accomplished. Therefore whoever relaxes one of the least of

---

Blomberg, "The Law in Luke-Acts," 72; Wells and Zaspel, _New Covenant Theology_, 153; Schreiner, _New Testament Theology_, 628.

[261] Reisinger, _Tablets of Stone_, 127.

[262] Graham A. Cole, _He Who Gives Life: The Doctrine of the Holy Spirit_ (Wheaton, IL: Crossway Books, 2007), 109-10.

[263] For book length treatments of this passage, see Gary Long, _Biblical Law and Ethics_. For a book length treatment of the "antitheses" that follow this passage, see John G. Reisinger, _But I Say Unto You_. Also see Wells and Zaspel, _New Covenant Theology_, 100ff.

these commandments and teaches others to do the same will be called least in the kingdom of heaven, but whoever does them and teaches them will be called great in the kingdom of heaven. For I tell you, unless your righteousness exceeds that of the scribes and Pharisees, you will never enter the kingdom of heaven (Matt 5:17-20).

The all-important word in this section is "fulfill" *(plēroō)*. Context is king in the task of exegesis. A very natural way to approach this word is to ask Matthew how he uses this word elsewhere. We don't have to look long before we encounter it in his quotations of the Old Testament (see Matt 1:22, 2:15, 17, 23, 4:14, 5:17, 8:17, 12:17, 13:35, 21:4, 26:54, 56, 27:9). Matthew is retelling Israel's history through the life of Jesus. Jesus fulfils all of the Old Testament. He "fills it up" by taking the story of Israel into himself.[264] N.T. Wright remarks:

> The gospels are therefore the story of Jesus *told as the history of Israel in miniature:* the 'typology' which is observed here and there by critics is simply a function of this larger purpose of the evangelists. Matthew gives us, in his first five chapters, a Genesis (1.1), and Exodus (2.15), and a Deuteronomy (5-7); he then gives us a royal and prophetic ministry, and finally an exile (the cross) and restoration (the resurrection).[265]

---

[264] J.R. Daniel Kirk, "Conceptualising Fulfilment in Matthew," *Tyndale Bulletin* 59, no. 1 (2008): 97.

[265] N.T Wright, *The New Testament and the People of God* (Minneapolis: Fortress Press, 1992), 402. It should be noted that while Bishop Wright is helpful in some of his writings, I would define the gospel quite differently than he would. I think the New Perspective on Paul is far from Pauline.

Like a new Moses, Jesus ascends the mountain (Matt 5:1), "replaying the law-giving moment in Israel's story."[266] Jesus came not to abolish the law but to bring about that which it pointed to. The law (and the prophets) pointed forward.[267] They *prophesied* (Matt 11:13, Rom 3:21).[268] Jesus fulfills the Law and the Prophets "in that they point to him, and he is their fulfillment."[269] Neither an iota nor a dot will pass from the Law until the Lord returns (Matt 5:18).[270] Some hold that only the moral law remains valid but Jesus' all-inclusive words here show that he means the law as a whole.[271] The "commandments" of verse nineteen refers to the Old Testament commandments interpreted through Christian lenses. Douglas Moo writes, "so 'these

---

[266] Kirk, "Conceptualising Fulfilment," 96.

[267] Moo notes, "Thus, it is suggested, as Jesus fulfilled the OT prophecies in his activity so he 'fulfilled' the OT law in his teaching," in "Jesus and the Authority of the Mosaic Law,"25.

[268] Blomberg, "The Law in Luke-Acts," 69, 71.

[269] Carson, *Matthew*, 143; So also Thielman, *Theology of the New Testament*, 88; Poythress, *The Shadow of Christ* (Phillipsburg, NJ: P & R Publishing, 1991), 265; Douglas J. Moo, "Jesus and the Authority of the Mosaic Law," *Journal for the Study of the New Testament* 20 (1984), 24-25; idem, "The Law of Moses or the Law of Christ," 205; idem, "The Law of Christ as the Fulfillment of the Law of Moses," 352; idem, "Law," in *DJG*, 457. Tom Wells and Fred Zaspel, *New Covenant Theology*, 109-22.

[270] Contra Don Garlington, who argues that the phrase "until heaven and earth pass away" (5:18) is apocalyptic metaphor to say that the Law "remains intact until such time as the new creation comes," in "Oath-Taking in the Community of the New Age," *Trinity Journal* 16, no. 2 (Fall 1995): 154-56

[271] Moo, "The Law of Moses or the Law of Christ," 206; Carson, *Matthew*, 143.

commandments' should be understood as referring to the commandments as fulfilled (and thereby, perhaps re-interpreted) in Jesus."[272] The antitheses of verses 21-48 bears this out.[273]

As we will see, there is no single interpretive paradigm that fits all six of these antitheses.[274] When Jesus says, "You have heard that it was said to those of old," "it is difficult to exclude some reference to the generation who received the law at Sinai."[275] In the first antithesis (5:21-26) concerning anger, Jesus is obviously quoting the sixth commandment: "You have heard that it was said to those of old, 'You shall not murder; and whoever murders will be liable to judgment.' But I say to you that everyone who is angry with his brother will be liable to judgment; whoever insults his brother will be liable to the council; and whoever says, 'You fool!' will be liable to the hell of fire" (Matt 5:21-22). After quoting the Old Testament, Jesus'

---

[272] Moo, "Jesus and the Authority of the Mosaic Law," 28; idem, "Law," in *DJG*, 457.

[273] D.A Carson writes, "The expression 'these commands' does not, I think, refer to the commands of the Old Testament law. It refers, rather, to the commands of the kingdom of heaven, the kingdom mentioned three times in verses 19f. They are the commands already given, and the commands still to come, in the Sermon on the Mount," *The Sermon on the Mount* (Grand Rapids: Baker Book House, 1978), 38. Contra Blomberg, *Matthew*, 105. Carson apparently changed his view to seeing them as the commandments of the OT Scriptures in *Matthew*, 146.

[274] Moo, "The Law of Christ as the Fulfillment of the Law of Moses," 350.

[275] Moo, "Jesus and the Mosaic Law," 18; idem, "The Law of Christ as fulfillment of the Law of Moses," 347.

"But I say to you" is clearly a contrast.[276] Some interpreters take Jesus as showing the true meaning of the law, however it is quite a leap from a call to not murder to a call not to be angry. Others say Jesus is deepening the law, which is true in part, but could be misleading. Jesus is not so much concerned with doing anything to the law. The emphatic "But I say to you" shows that here Jesus is concerned with laying down his own authoritative kingdom ethic.[277]

The next antithesis (Matt 5:27-30) is much the same: "You have heard that it was said, 'You shall not commit adultery.' But I say to you that everyone who looks at a woman with lustful intent has already committed adultery with her in his heart" (Matt 5:27-28). Here Jesus quotes the seventh commandment but transcends the Mosaic teaching by prohibiting lust.[278]

In the third antithesis (Matt 5:31-32), Jesus teaches that divorce, except on the ground of sexual immorality, is adultery, and whoever marries a divorced woman commits adultery: "It was also said, 'Whoever divorces his wife, let him give her a certificate of divorce.' But I say to you that everyone who divorces his wife, except on the ground of

---

[276] The "I" is emphatic (*egō de legō*). Nelson, "Christian Morality," 8 n.9; Reisinger, *But I Say Unto You*, 42; Frank Thielman, *Theology of the New Testament* (Grand Rapids: Zondervan, 2005), 87; idem, *The Law and the New Testament*, 52f.

[277] Moo, "The Law of Christ as the Fulfillment of the Law of Moses," 349.

[278] Stephen Westerholm, "The Law in the Sermon on the Mount," *Criswell Theological Review* 6, no. 1 (Fall 1992): 53; Moo, "Law," in *DJG*, 455.

sexual immorality, makes her commit adultery. And
whoever marries a divorced woman commits adultery. In
this passage, Jesus is referring to Deuteronomy 24:1-4 and
his teaching is clearly more exacting than Deuteronomy.[279]

In the fourth antithesis (Matt 5:33-37), Jesus does not
directly quote the Old Testament, but summarizes a
number of passages about truth-telling (Exodus 20:7,
Leviticus 19:12, Numbers 30:2, and Deuteronomy 5:11):[280]
"Again you have heard that it was said to those of old,
'You shall not swear falsely, but shall perform to the Lord
what you have sworn.' But I say to you, Do not take an
oath at all, either by heaven, for it is the throne of God, or
by the earth, for it is his footstool, or by Jerusalem, for it is
the city of the great King" (Matt 5:33-35). Here Jesus clearly
forbids what the Old Testament permits, namely oaths.[281]
D.A. Carson writes, "It must be frankly admitted that here
Jesus formally contravenes OT law."[282]

In the fifth antithesis (Matt 5:38-42), Jesus alludes to
Exodus 21:24, Deuteronomy 19:21, and Leviticus 24:19-20:
"You have heard that it was said, 'An eye for an eye and a
tooth for a tooth.' But I say to you, Do not resist the one

---

[279] Blomberg, *Matthew*, 110; Moo says that Jesus goes beyond the OT in
this passage, "Jesus and the Mosaic Law," 20; Moo, "Law," in *DJG*,
456.

[280] Carson, *Matthew*, 153.

[281] Blomberg, *Matthew*, 112

[282] Carson, 154. Moo agrees: Jesus does not exposit or deepen the
commandment, but effectively cancels legislation which is no longer
needed since the practice it regulated is prohibited in the coming
Age," "Jesus and the Mosaic Law," 21.

who is evil. But if anyone slaps you on the right cheek, turn
to him the other also. And if anyone would sue you and
take your tunic, let him have your cloak as well. And if
anyone forces you to go one mile, go with him two miles.
Give to the one who begs from you, and do not refuse the
one who would borrow from you." Here again, Jesus
"formally abrogates an Old Testament command in order
to intensify and internalize its application."[283]

In the sixth and final antithesis (Matt 5:43-48), Jesus says,
"You have heard that it was said, 'You shall love your
neighbor and hate your enemy.' But I say to you, Love
your enemies and pray for those who persecute you" (Matt
5:43-44). In the first part of the verse, it is clear that Jesus is
again quoting Leviticus 19:18, but there seems to be no Old
Testament command to hate your enemy.[284] This final
antithesis is the only one with a quotation that isn't from
the Old Testament.[285] Jesus concludes the antitheses with

---

[283] Blomberg, *Matthew*, 113; Carson, *Matthew*, 155. Schreiner argues that
Jesus is countering a misinterpretation of the law here, and that
Jesus is speaking against the practice of applying the judicial
principle of the *lex talionis* to the personal sphere, *New Testament
Theology*, 630. So also Moo, "Jesus and the Mosaic Law," 22. But as
Carson notes, "But it will not do to argue that Jesus is doing nothing
more than combating a personal as opposed to a judicial use of the
lex talionis, since in that case the examples would necessarily run
differently: e.g., if someone strikes you, don't strike back but let the
judiciary administer the just return slap. The argument runs in
deeper channels," *Matthew*, 155.

[284] See John Reisinger, *But I Say Unto You*, 81-92, who shows that it may
have been Deuteronomy 23:6 (You shall not seek their peace or their
prosperity all your days for ever) that Jesus was alluding to.

[285] Blomberg, *Matthew*, 114; Moo, "Jesus and the Mosaic Law," 22;
Carson, *Matthew*, 157.

verse 48: "You therefore must be perfect, as your heavenly Father is perfect."

What should be clear from this passage is that the locus of authority has shifted from the Mosaic law to the law of Christ in the new age. He is the authoritative one.[286] He *contrasts* his teaching with the teaching of Moses.[287] Daniel Kirk is worth quoting at length,

> With only one possible exception, Jesus does not cite what he takes to be errant interpretations of the laws and set his interpretation over against the customary reading; he sets his own teaching as a counterpoint to the law itself. Moreover, Matthew's summary comment indicates that his intention in the Sermon was to portray Jesus as one speaking from his own authority in contrast to the scribes (7:29). The difference is not simply that Jesus is giving a better, more challenging interpretation, but that he is setting himself up as a teacher with his own authority, not an authority derived from the subject matter of the law.[288]

So we see that the whole canon, interpreted in light of Jesus Christ and the new covenant, is our authority. This raises an important question. What is the relation between the law of Moses and the law of Christ?

---

[286] Moo, "Law" in *DJG*, 453.

[287] Westerholm, "The Law in the Sermon on the Mount," 52-53; C.G. Kruse, "Law," in *NDBT*, 634.

[288] Kirk, "Conceptualising Fulfilment," 96.

CHAPTER 12

THE LAW OF CHRIST IN
RELATION TO THE LAW OF MOSES:
DISCONTINUITY

It should be clear that there is significant continuity *and* discontinuity between the law of Moses and the law of Christ. The law of Christ is new, but it is not absolutely new. There is overlap. We see that all the Law and Prophets are applicable to new covenant believers, but only as they are interpreted in light of their fulfillment (Matt 5:17). Craig Blomberg writes, "The Old Testament remains normative and relevant for Jesus' followers (2 Tim 3:16), but none of it can rightly be interpreted until one understands how it has been fulfilled in Christ. Every Old Testament text must be viewed in light of Jesus' person and ministry and the changes introduced by the new covenant he inaugurated."[289] We read all of Scripture with Christian lenses on. Jesus is our hermeneutical filter.

Discontinuity

---

[289] Blomberg, *Matthew*, 104; Moo agrees: "the continuing validity of the law is to be understood in the light of its 'fulfillment' (v. 17). In all its details, the Scripture remains authoritative, but the manner in which men are to relate to and understand its provisions is now determined by the one who has fulfilled it," "Jesus and the Mosaic Law," 27.

First we will look at discontinuity. The law of Christ is not totally distinct from the law of Moses, but it is _new_.[290] As early as the 150's AD, Justin Martyr called Christ the "new Lawgiver."[291] As we have seen, Paul clearly distinguished between the law of Moses and the law of Christ. He is not under the law of Moses, but under the law of Christ (1 Cor 9:20-21). Keeping the commands of God is no longer keeping the Mosaic law (which included circumcision) according to 1 Corinthians 7:19. God's law has shifted from the law of Moses in the old covenant to the law of Christ in the new. We do not look directly to Moses. "We have our own master, Christ, and he has set before us what we are to know, observe, do, and leave undone."[292]

---

[290] Thielman, Paul and the Law, 141.

[291] Martyr, Justin, Dialougue with Trypho, trans. Thomas B. Falls (Washington, D.C.: The Catholic University of America Press, 2003), 24. Similarly, The Epistle of Barnabas (ca. 80-120 AD) speaks of "the New Law of our Lord Jesus Christ," Early Christian Writings. Penguin Classics (Penguin Books: New York, 1968), 160.

[292] Luther, "How Christians Should Regard Moses," in Martin Luther's Basic Theological Writings, 147-48. He also writes, "Moses is dead. His rule ended when Christ came. He is of no further service," ibid., 139. Elsewhere he says, "For since God here promises another Moses whom they are to hear, it follows of necessity that this other one would teach something different from Moses; and Moses gives up his power and yield to him, so that men will listen to him. This [coming] prophet cannot, then, teach the law, for Moses has done that to perfection; for the law's sake there would be no need to raise up another prophet. Therefore this word was surely spoken concerning Christ and the teaching of grace," "Preface to the Old Testament," in Martin Luther's Basic Theological Writings, 129.

Some scholars argue that the law of Christ mentioned in Galatians 6:2 must be a reference to the Mosaic law because Galatians 5:14 (For the whole law is fulfilled in one word: You shall love your neighbor as yourself) is clearly referring to the law of Moses.[293] But Paul adds an all-important genitive descriptor to the phrase "law;" it is the law *of Christ (ton nomon tou Christou)*! Moreover, after spending half the letter showing how the law was temporary and believers are no longer under it, he surely would have confused the Galatians by concluding with "Oh, by the way, you are still to fulfill the Mosaic law." Also, the ultimate context of any given passage is the whole canon. When looking at the teaching of the New Testament, it seems highly unlikely that Galatians 6:2 is referring to the law of Moses instead of the law of Christ. It is also important to point out that two different verbs are used in these verses, which is almost certainly deliberate. Galatians 5:14 uses *plēroō* while 6:2 uses *anaplēroō*.[294]

---

[293] E.g. Todd A. Wilson, writes, "the proximity of 5.13-14 and 6.2 within the epistle makes it highly unlikely that Paul would have intended to refer to something other than the law of Moses in 6.2, when he has just said virtually the exact same thing a few verses earlier (5.13-14)," in "The Law of Christ and the Law of Moses: Reflections on a Recent Trend in Interpretation," *Currents in Biblical Research* 5, no. 1 (October 2006), 135. Stanton also holds this position in "The Law of Moses and the Law of Christ," 116.

[294] Fee writes, "In the one case Torah has been fulfilled so as no longer to obtain; in this case 'the law of Christ' is 'fulfilled' in every case where in love believers bear each others' burdens. Thus the 'fulfillment' in the fist instance is almost certainly to be understood in light of its further 'being filled to the full' by those who,

Another reason it is clear that the law of Christ is not the same as the law of Moses is the glaring lack of direct appeal to the law, especially when it would have been very easy to do so.[295] For example, he could have easily quoted Exodus 20:14 or Leviticus 18-20 (on sexual immorality) to the Thessalonians if he believed it was the eternal moral law of God. But he doesn't proceed that way. Rather, he says, "For this is the will of God, your sanctification: that you abstain from sexual immorality; that each of you know how to control his own body in holiness and honor, not in the passion of lust like the Gentiles who do not know God" (1 Thess 4:3-5, cf. also Eph 5:3-5). First Corinthians is similar; Paul doesn't go to the Decalogue, but instead uses gospel logic: "Do you not know that your bodies are members of Christ?" (1 Cor 6:15a). To the Ephesians, Paul could have quoted Exodus 20:16 (Do not lie), but instead he says, "Let the thief no longer steal, but rather let him labor" (Eph 4:28a).

When teaching on idolatry, Paul does not go to the First or Second Commandments (see 1 Cor 10:14-22, Eph 5:5, Col 3:5) when he easily could have. It is quite shocking that he does not! Also, in Philemon, Paul, in returning Onesimus to Philemon "fails" to mention Deuteronomy 23:15-16, which reads, "You shall not give up to his master a slave who has escaped from his master to you. He shall dwell with you, in

empowered by the Spirit, so live as Christ himself did," *God's Empowering Presence*, 463-64.

[295] Seifrid, *Christ, Our Righteousness*, 126; Deidun, *New Covenant Morality*, 157-60, who notes that Paul never appealed to the prescriptions of the law as a basis of Christian obligation; so also Meyer, *The End of the Law*, 283.

your midst, in the place that he shall choose within one of
your towns, wherever it suits him. You shall not wrong
him."[296] As Westerholm writes, "Paul never derives
appropriate Christian conduct simply and directly by
applying pertinent command in Torah – the inevitable
procedure if Torah remained the binding statement of
God's will for believers."[297]

Do/Fulfill

Also of importance is the way Paul carefully
distinguishes the verbs "do" and "fulfill" in terms of the
believer's relation to the law.[298] Stephen Westerholm
writes,

---

[296] Seifrid, Christ Our Righteousness, 126 n102.

[297] Westerholm, "On Fulfilling the Whole Law," 232-33. Elsewhere, he
writes, "It is, moreover, striking (and has struck many) that Paul
repeatedly refrains from citing prohibitions from the law even when
dealing with basic issues related to idolatry or sexual morality,
opting instead to argue from Christian principles (e.g., 1 Cor 6:12-
20; 10:14-22; 1 Thess 4:3-8). And when Paul speaks of the need for
Christians to discern the will of God, he does not refer them to the
law (though, according to Rom. 2:18, the law provided Jews with
guidance about God's will), but speaks rather of presenting
themselves to God, of refusing to pattern their way of life after that
of this age, of being 'transformed by the renewal of [their] mind[s]'
(12:2). They 'approve what is excellent' (the same phrase as in 2:18 is
used of Christians in Phil. 1:9-10) when their love grows in
knowledge and judgment. The fact that Jews had to discover the
will of God in the statutes of Torah but Christians must discover it
as their minds are 'renewed' and they grow in insight shows clearly
that the will of God is no longer defined as an obligation to observe
the statues of the Mosaic law," Perspectives, 432-33.

[298] I do not think Romans 2:13-14 is referring to Christians. I think
Christians are not mentioned until 2:28.

It is worth noting, however, that in Paul, while Christians are never said to "do" (*poiein*) the law, those "under the law" are seen as obligated to "do" its commands (Rom. 10:5; Gal. 3:10, 12; 5:3); indeed, the law itself, Paul claims, rests on the principle of "doing" as opposed to "believing" (Gal. 3:12; Rom. 10:5-6). If, then, the essence of life "under the law" is the requirement to "do" its commands, it is not strange that Paul would avoid the term in contexts where he relates Christian behavior to the law. On the other hand, where specifically Christian behavior is related positively to the Mosaic law, the verb *plēroun* or a cognate inevitably occurs (Rom. 8:4, 13:8, 10; Gal. 5:14); yet these terms are *never* used where the requirements or achievements of those living "under the law" are in view. Given the occasional nature of Paul's correspondence, such a consistent distinction in usage is striking indeed and demands some explanation.[299]

Galatians 5:14, "For the whole law is *fulfilled* in one word: You shall love your neighbor as yourself." In Romans 8:4, the righteous requirement (*to dikaiōma*) of the law is *fulfilled* in us. I still think (with Calvin) that the righteous requirement of the law is fulfilled in us because of the objective work of Christ on our behalf, rather than being fulfilled by the obedience of Christians (i.e. those who walk

---

[299] Stephen Westerholm, "On Fulfilling the Whole Law (Gal. 5:14)," *Svensk exegetisk årsbok* 51-52 (1986-87): 233-34; idem, *Perspectives New and Old*, 329, 435-39; Longenecker, *Galatians*, 242-43; Moo writes, "Vital to understanding Paul's perspective on the law is to recognize a principial distinction in his writings between 'doing' and 'fulfilling' the law. Nowhere does Paul say that Christians are to 'do' the law, and nowhere does he suggest that any but Christian can 'fulfill' the law," "The Law of Christ as the Fulfillment of the Law of Moses," 359; idem, "The Law of Moses or the Law of Christ," 210.

according to the flesh).[300] Four reasons lead me to this conclusion: First, the context is primarily judicial. Three verses earlier Paul proclaimed that there is now no condemnation for those in Christ. The previous verse says that God has done what the law could not do, by sending his Son to condemn sin in the flesh *in order that* the *dikaiōma* of the law might be fulfilled in us. Second, the way Paul uses this word in other places in Romans (see 1:32, 2:26, 5:16, 5:18, 8:4). Romans 5:16 and 5:18 are most significant for me: "And the free gift is not like the result of that one man's sin. For the judgment following one trespass brought condemnation, but the free gift following many trespasses brought justification (*dikaiōma*)...Therefore, as one trespass led to condemnation for all men, so one act of righteousness (*dikaiōmatos*) leads to justification and life for all men." Third, sinners never fulfill this righteous requirement (note the singular). Calvin writes, "For the faithful, while they sojourn in this world, never make such a proficiency, as that the justification [*dikaiōma*] of the law becomes in them full or complete. This then must be applied to forgiveness; for when the obedience of Christ is accepted for us, the law is satisfied, so that we are counted just."[301] Fourth, as Douglas Moo points out, "the passive verb 'might *be* fulfilled' points not to something that we are to do but to something that is done in and for us...we may

---

[300] Contra Fee, *God's Empowering Presence*, 534-38; Schreiner, *Romans*, 406, who says, "Those who confine obedience to forensic categories in 8:4 seem to miss rather badly the scope of Paul's argument."

[301] Calvin, John, *Commentaries on the Epistle of Paul the Apostle to the Romans*, trans. John Owen (Grand Rapids: Baker Book House, 2005), 283.

interpret 'the righteous requirement of the law' to be the demand of the law for perfect obedience, or for righteousness. And the law's just demand is fulfilled in Christians not through their own acts of obedience but through their incorporation into Christ. He fulfilled the law; and, in him, believers also fulfill the law—perfectly, so that they may be pronounced 'righteous,' free from 'condemnation' (v. 1)."[302]

Also in Romans 13:8 we are told "the one who loves another has fulfilled the law." Verse ten says "love is the fulfilling of the law." Only Christians, who have the Spirit of the new age, can fulfill the law. Paul, like Jesus in Matthew 5:17, is referring to eschatological fulfillment.[303] It should also not be overlooked that in these "fulfillment of the law" passages, Paul is not prescribing but describing Christian behavior.[304] Jason Meyer states, "Paul does not prescribe Christian behavior with reference to the law; he describes the 'fruit' (*karpos*) of their behavior with a retroactive reference to the way that it conforms to the law

---

[302] Moo, *Romans*, 483-84.

[303] Fee, *God's Empowering Presence*, 614. Moo writes, "Paul is thinking about a complete and final 'doing' of the law that is possible only in the new age of eschatological accomplishment," *Romans*, 814.

[304] Westerholm writes, "When Paul *prescribes* what Christians are to do, the language used is not that of fulfilling the Mosaic law. 'Walk by the Spirit, and do not gratify the desires of the flesh' (5:16; cf. Rom. 8:12-13). Naturally, it is from Paul's *prescriptions* that we must derive his view of the basis for Christian obligation. When, on the other hand, Christian ethics is related to the Mosaic law in the fulfillment passages, the view is retrospective. Paul's purpose is to provide assurance of the quality of Christian conduct, not to define its several duties," *Perspectives*, 434-35.

and thus amounts to its 'fulfillment' (*plēroō*). Ironically and paradoxically, those who live under the law bear fruit resulting in sinful passions, transgression of the law, and death, while those who have died to the law bear fruit that amount to the law's fulfillment."[305] Only those under the law are *required* to *do* the law, while the *result* of the obedience of those not under the law *fulfills* the law.[306]

Hebrews

Hebrews is an important book with regard to discontinuity between the Testaments.[307] It could be summed up as "Jesus is better." The sermon begins "Long ago, at many times and in many ways, God spoke to our fathers by the prophets, but in these last days he has spoken to us by his Son" (1:1-2a). Here we already have a hint of contrast between Jesus and Moses in the first verse of Hebrews since Moses was considered the greatest of the prophets, who are inferior to the Son, through whom God has spoken with finality. Then the preacher shows Jesus' superiority to angels. This is another way of saying that the Son's revelation is superior to the revelation given at Sinai for there was plenty of Jewish tradition which associated angels with the giving of the law (Deut 33:2 LXX, Gal 3:19, Acts 7:38, 53, Heb 2:2).[308]

---

[305] Meyer, The End of the Law, 283.

[306] Westerholm, "On Fulfilling the Whole Law," 235.

[307] I am borrowing material from my The Newness of the New Covenant (Frederick, MD: New Covenant Media, 2008) for this section on Hebrews.

[308] Stanton, "The Law of Moses and the Law of Christ," 113; Westerholm, Perspectives, 413.

Then Hebrews presents Christ as the true human (Ps 8, Gen 1:26-28). God's intention from the start was to rule the world through a faithful humanity, but where is the faithful humanity? We see *him* who restores our humanity by tasting death for everyone and destroying the devil (2:5-18). Next, Jesus, the *Son* who is faithful *over* God's house, is presented as greater than Moses, a faithful *servant in* God's house (3:5-6). Jesus is also greater than Joshua (3:7-4:13). Joshua led the people into the land and seemingly had rest (Josh 21:43-45), but much later David wrote, "Today, if you hear his voice, do not harden your hearts" (3:7 quoting Ps 95). "For if Joshua had given them rest, God would not have spoken of another day later on" (Heb 4:8). An eschatological Sabbath rest still awaited the people of God and Jesus has brought Sabbath rest for those who trust him *today*. One thinks of the famous passage in Matthew 11.28-30 where Jesus says, "Come to me, all who labor and are heavy laden, and I will give you rest," which is immediately followed by the passage in chapter twelve (an unfortunate chapter break) where Jesus proclaims himself as Lord of the Sabbath.

Next the author of Hebrews begins to show how Jesus fulfills the Levitical priesthood (5:1-10), but pauses to warn the people of the dangers of not persevering. It picks back up the teaching concerning Christ's priesthood in chapter seven. He begins by making a few exegetical comments on Genesis 14:17-20, and then shows how Melchizedek, priestly-king of (Jeru)Salem blessed Abraham and received a tithe from him, making Melchizedek superior. Melchizedek also lacks a genealogy, which is a very significant literary observation in the text of Genesis.[309] Since Levi was not even born yet, he in some sense paid tithes to Melchizedek, again showing the superiority of the Melchizedekian priestly order that has no end.

Hebrews 7:11-12 are crucial verses: "Now if perfection was through the Levitical priesthood (for on the basis of it the people received the Law), what further need *was there* for another priest to arise according to the order of Melchizedek, and not be designated according to the order of Aaron? For when the priesthood is changed, of necessity there takes place a change of law also" (NASB).[310] The change in redemptive history brings a change in the locus of authority. The duration of the law is bound up with the duration of the covenant of which it is a part. Notice first that the old covenant must be seen as a package (as we have seen). On the basis of the priesthood the people received the law. It is a whole unit, consisting of law, covenant, and priesthood. Dividing the law covenant up is foreign to the Bible.[311] You can't divorce a covenant from its

---

[309] See Genesis 2:4, 5:1, 6:9, 10:1, 11:10, 11:27, 25:12, 25:19, 36:1, 36:9, 37:2.

[310] I use the NASB here because the ESV's translation is unfortunate. The ESV translates verse 12: "For when there is a change in the priesthood, there is necessarily a change in the law as well." Both "law" (*nomou*) and "priesthood" (hierōsynēs) are in the genitive case, not the dative. It is not a change *in* the law, but a change *of* law. See Long, *Biblical Law and Ethics,* 54 n58. The KJV, NET, NLT, and NIV are better than the ESV on this verse.

[311] Some appeal to Matthew 23:23, where Jesus rebukes the Pharisees for neglecting the weightier matters of the law, but this proves too much because in the very same passage Jesus insists that they should have done all of them. We must read in context, which obviously starts with reading the whole verse.

law. The law is contained within the covenant as we saw in Exodus 19-24. Also note that the Text says that when the priesthood is changed (which there clearly is), there is necessarily *a change of law* as well. The Spirit-inspired Word says that there is a change of the law (not change *in* the law as the ESV translates it). New Covenant Theology is not making this stuff up. We are seeking to do justice to the inscripturated Text. Also note, as mentioned above, that God never intended for the old covenant to bring ultimate salvation (perfection). This is why David, hundreds of years after Genesis 14, wrote of a new priestly order to come: "You are a priest forever, after the order of Melchizedek" (Heb 7:17 quoting Ps 110). "On the one hand, a former commandment is set aside because of its weakness and uselessness (for the law made nothing perfect); but on the other hand, a better hope is introduced, through which we draw near to God" (7:18-19). The former commandment is set aside. Since the law-covenant was a package deal, Christ not only brings a new priesthood, but is also "guarantor of a better covenant" (7:22), as we saw above when dealing with chapter eight.

Hebrews agrees with Paul and Jesus that the old covenant law was intended to be an interim covenant, merely a shadow (*skia*) of the good things to come instead of the true form of these realities (Heb 10:1, cf. Col 2:17). The argument of Hebrews is that the Jew should have understood the self-confessed inadequacy of the old order (Ps 8, 95, 110, Jer 31). The law of Christ is a new law.

Sabbath

Finally, (as with circumcision) the Sabbath command is abrogated in the New Testament. This command creates problems for those who believe that the Ten Commandments are directly binding on believers. The New Testament is clear that we are no longer bound to obey the Sabbath command. The Sabbath was the sign of the old covenant, which has passed away with the death and resurrection of Christ. So just as believers are no longer bound to the old covenant, neither are they bound to the sign of that covenant.[312] Jesus, as Lord of the Sabbath, is above the law (Luke 6:1-11, Mark 2:23-28). Matthew's account is significant in that Jesus' claim as Lord of the Sabbath follows his invitation to the heavy-laden to come and receive rest (Matt 11:28-30, cf. also John 5:1-19).

As we saw above, the book of Hebrews views the Sabbath as a type of the eschatological rest brought about by Jesus (Heb 3:7-4:11). For new covenant believers, the command to obey the Sabbath is a command to believe the gospel. Colossians 2:16-17 says, "Therefore let no one pass judgment on you in questions of food and drink, or with regard to a festival or a new moon or a Sabbath. These are a shadow of the things to come, but the substance belongs to Christ." This verse is crystal clear, if we will let Paul say what he says. Paul relegates the Sabbath to a shadow (skia), making it highly unlikely that he viewed the Sabbath as being fulfilled in the Lord's Day.[313] There is simply no

---

[312] Reisinger, Tablets of Stone, 72-81; Schreiner, 40 Questions, 249.

[313] Moo, Colossians, 224. On 2:17, he comments, "According to the fundamental salvation-historical perspective of the New Testament writers, the Old Testament, and especially the law, belonged to the time of promise, to the time when God was preparing his people and the world for salvation in Christ. With the coming of Christ, the new era of fulfillment has dawned. The old era and the law have

biblical or early historical evidence for viewing the Lord's Day as a fulfillment of the Sabbath.[314]

Romans 14:5-6a says, "One person esteems one day as better than another, while another esteems all days alike. Each one should be fully convinced in his own mind. The one who observes the day, observes it in honor of the Lord." The days in mind here would certainly include the Sabbath. As Tom Schreiner writes, "Any Jew would inevitably think of the Sabbath, for this was the day that most distinguished the Jews from others."[315] This is a far cry from "Remember the Sabbath day, to keep it holy. Six days you shall labor, and do all your work, but the seventh day is a Sabbath to the LORD your God. On it you shall not do any work, you, or your son, or your daughter, your male servant, or your female servant, or your livestock, or the sojourner who is within your gates" (Exod 20:8-10).

Finally, in Galatians 4:8-11, Paul can go so far as to deem observing Jewish days (the Sabbath would certainly be included), months and seasons and years for their justification as returning to the weak and worthless elemental spirits of the world, i.e. demonic forces (see the exegesis above)!

---

now been brought to their 'culmination' (Rom. 10:4). Believers who belong to the new era through their incorporation into Christ therefore experience the reality to which the Old Testament and its law pointed. And they are no longer compelled to follow the laws of that earlier era," 223.

[314] See the essays in *From Sabbath to Lord's Day: A Biblical, Historical, and Theological Investigation*, ed. D.A. Carson (Grand Rapids: Zondervan, 1982); A.G. Shead, "Sabbath," in *NDBT*, 749-50.

[315] Schreiner, *Romans*, 715; so also Moo, *Romans*, 842.

CHAPTER 13

THE LAW OF CHRIST IN RELATION TO THE LAW OF MOSES: CONTINUITY

Having seen that there is a heavy dose of discontinuity, we will now look at the continuity between the law of Moses and the law of Christ. So, although new covenant believers are not under the Mosaic law, with Jesus and the new covenant Scriptures as our hermeneutical filter, *every* command in Scripture remains applicable.[316] In this sense, we can receive *principles* from the old covenant law.[317] A common example is that of bestiality. Some argue that New Covenant Theologians have no theological grounding for excluding such a practice. While the word *sexual immorality* (*porneia*) is probably broad enough to include such a practice, I have no problem appealing to Exodus 22:19, Leviticus 18:23, 20:16. I interpret these passage, like all Old Testament commands, in light of Jesus Christ.

I think a legitimate application of Deuteronomy 22:8 (When you build a new house, you shall make a parapet

---

[316] Frank Thielman writes that the Mosaic law continues to be authoritative when "interpreted through the eschatological lens of the gospel," *The Law and the New Testament,* 35.

[317] Kruse writes, "While believers were not obliged to carry out all the demands of the Mosaic law, they could nevertheless draw from the OT, read paradigmatically, lessons for Christian living, "Law," *NDBT,* 636.

for your roof, that you may not bring the guilt of blood upon your house, if anyone should fall from it) for a new covenant believer would be to ensure that their property is not a danger to their neighbors. The common example is to build a fence around your swimming pool. Exodus 22:25 calls Israel not to charge interest when lending money to fellow Israelites. For us, we can apply this by being generous and open-handed with fellow believers (and obviously not charge interest when lending).[318] Doug Moo writes, "A Christian reading the laws about personal injury in Exodus 21 might well conclude—rightly, I think—that the killing of an unborn baby falls into the category of those takings of human life that are prohibited by both the Decalogue and by the New Testament. The detailed stipulations of the Mosaic law often reveal principles that are part of God's word to his people in both covenants, and believers continue to profit from what the law teaches in this respect."[319] Most of us do not have a field and hence cannot leave the fallen grapes for the poor and for the sojourner (Lev 19:9-10), but we obey the principle behind this command: care for the poor and be hospitable to strangers, which is another way of saying we should love your neighbor (Lev 19:18). Examples such as these could go on and on.

Paul seems to be "principalizing" the law in 1 Corinthians 9:9-10a: "For it is written in the Law of Moses, 'You shall not muzzle an ox when it treads out the grain.' Is it for oxen that God is concerned? Does he not speak

---

[318] David A. Dorsey, "The Law of Moses and the Christian," 333.

[319] Moo, "The of Law of Christ as the Fulfillment of the Law of Moses," 376.

entirely for our sake?"[320] Here Paul draws out a principle from Deuteronomy 25:4. Paul is not imposing the law on new covenant believers. In fact, he is remarkably free with his use of the passage. He is using it to summarize a principle: the worker should reap material benefit from his work.[321]

We find nine of the Ten Commandments reiterated in the New Testament. The Sabbath command is the issue that divides theological systems. But as we have seen, the Ten Commandments cannot be extrapolated from the rest of the old covenant. The quotation of the Fifth Commandment in Ephesians 6:2 demonstrates that while there is significant discontinuity, there is also continuity. In this same letter, Paul had already said that Christ had "abolished the law of commandments expressed in ordinances" (2:15) yet he can go on later to quote this very law. The command to honor one's parents is both part of the law of Moses and part of the law of Christ (because, as we will see, it is part of God's natural law).[322] It should also be noted though, that the Fifth Commandment does not come over unchanged. As Peter O'Brien notes, "Significantly, when Paul 'reapplies' the commandment to his Christian readers, he omits any reference to the land of

---

[320] See also Paul's use of the OT in 1 Cor 14:34 and Gal 4:21-31.

[321] Deidun, *New Covenant Morality*, 158. Fee, *The Epistle to the Corinthians*, 407 n59; Moo, "The Law of Moses or the Law of Christ," 216; Westerholm, "On Fulfilling the Whole Law," 232 n12; idem, *Perspectives*, 435 n64.

[322] Moo, "The Law of Moses or the Law of Christ," 216; idem, "The Law of Christ as the Fulfillment of the Law of Moses," 370; O'Brien, *Ephesians*, 444.

Israel and 'universalizes' the promise: 'that it may go well with you and that you may enjoy long life on the earth'."[323]

As we have seen, even though we are no longer bound to the Mosaic law, the whole canon, the Decalogue included, is relevant for new covenant believers. It witnesses to Christ. It shows us our sin. It reveals the character of our great God and king. In his important article, David Dorsey writes,

> Legally, none of the 613 stipulations of the Sinaitic covenant are binding upon NT Christians, including the so-called moral laws, while in a revelatory and pedagogical sense all 613 are binding upon us, including all the ceremonial and civic laws...the Mosaic Laws, though not legally binding, comprise a treasure of insights and information regarding the very mind and ways of God... it was tailor-made by the One we seek to know and serve. It is here that the point of profound applicability for the Christian is found. A law reflects the mind, the personality, the priorities, the values, the likes and dislikes of the lawgiver. Each law issued by God to ancient Israel (like each declaration by God through the prophets) reflects God's mind and ways and is therefore a theological treasure.[324]

---

[323] O'Brien, *Ephesians*, 444. Paul is probably here referring to the new creation, the new earth, not a small piece of real estate with national boundaries. See Frank Thielman, "Ephesians," in *Commentary on the New Testament Use of the Old*, 830.

[324] David A. Dorsey, "The Law of Moses and the Christian," 325, 332. C.G. Kruse similarly writes, "The law continued to have an educative role for them, but it was no longer the regulatory norm under which they lived. Christians were not bound to the actual demands of the law but had much to learn from the principles and values underlying them," "Law," in *NDBT*, 636. Meyer writes, "The

The law and the prophets are applicable to new covenant believers interpreted in light of Christ.[325] Jason Meyer puts it well: "The coming of Christ has caused a paradigm shift that calls for recalibrating all former commands in the light of His centrality. This approach recognizes that the law of Moses in its entirety has come to an end in the sense that the believer does not start by asking, 'What did the law teach?' The believer begins at the point where his Christian life began: Christ. The believer found new life in Christ and so now comes to Christ to find out how to live out his new life."[326]

---

law remains as a vibrant demonstration of God's character and wisdom," *The End of the Law,* 286.

[325] Moo writes, "The law remains authoritative for the disciple of Jesus only insofar as it is taken up into his own teaching," "Law," in *DJG,* 461. Elsewhere he writes, "The *whole* law, every 'jot and tittle,' is fulfilled in Christ and can only be understood and applied in light of that fulfillment," in "The Law of Moses or the Law of Christ," 218.

[326] Meyer, *The End of the Law,* 283.

CHAPTER 14

NATURAL LAW

The Westminster Larger Catechism famously states, "The moral law is summarily comprehended in the ten commandments."[327] As we have seen, this assertion cannot be sustained by exegesis. God indeed has "an eternal moral law," but it cannot be the Ten Commandments since they are bound up with a *temporary* covenant. What then is this moral law? Wells and Zaspel define moral law as "the law that has its source in the unchanging moral character of God with the result that it is intrinsically right and therefore binds all men of every era and every land to whom it comes."[328] Due to the baggage the term "moral law" brings, I prefer to call it the "natural law" (following Luther) although it is not without its baggage as well. Such is the case in theology this side of the *parousia*. Moo refers to this truth as "God's eternal moral will."[329] New Covenant Theologian Gary Long calls it "absolute law."[330]

---

[327] *The Westminster Confession of Faith* (Atlanta: Committee for Christian Education & Publications, 1990), 54; Horton, *Introducing Covenant Theology*, 178.

[328] Wells and Zaspel, *New Covenant Theology*, 162.

[329] Moo, "The Law of Christ as the Fulfillment of the Law of Moses," 370.

[330] Long writes, "God's absolute law ethically and morally binds all mankind as individuals whether before or after the cross," in *Biblical Law and Ethics: Absolute and Covenantal*, 85-86.

The natural law is written on the heart of all people by nature.[331] In Romans 1, Paul writes, "For the wrath of God is revealed from heaven against all ungodliness and unrighteousness of men, who by their unrighteousness suppress the truth. For what can be known about God is plain to them, because God has shown it to them" (18-19). "Though they know God's decree (*dikaiōma*) that those who practice such things deserve to die, they not only do them but give approval to those who practice them" (32). In Romans 2:26, Paul uses this same word "*dikaiōma*": "So, if a man who is uncircumcised keeps the precepts (*dikaiōmata*) of the law, will not his uncircumcision be regarded as circumcision?" In Romans 2:14-15, Paul writes, "For when Gentiles, who do not have the law, by nature do what the law requires, they are a law to themselves, even though they do not have the law. They show that the work of the law is written on their hearts, while their conscience also bears witness, and their conflicting thoughts accuse or even excuse them." God's decree is known to all. All have the work of the law written on their hearts. Natural law is grounded in creation and expresses God's character.

The heart of natural law, just like the heart of the Mosaic law and the law of Christ is love. This is why the so-called "Golden Rule" is universal.[332] Matthew 7:12 says, "So

---

[331] Luther, "How Christians Should Regard Moses," 138.

[332] Charles Leiter, "The Law – Its Essence vs. Its Implications," http://www.todaysamericandream.com/TheLawCharlesLeiter.pdf. Calvin wrote, "We render to our neighbors what belongs to them and observe *the natural law* of not doing anything to anyone unless we would want them to do the same to us," *The Soul of Life: The Piety of John Calvin* ed. by Joel R. Beeke (Grand Rapids: Reformation Heritage Books, 2009), 205.

whatever you wish that others would do to you, do also to them, for this is the Law and the Prophets." One can find some form of it in every religion. People know by nature they should love God and neighbor, but because they are in Adam they suppress it.

This natural law comes from God in various forms.[333] It comes through conscience and the created order, through the law of Moses in the old covenant, and through the Law of Christ in the new covenant.[334] We see this from our important passage 1 Corinthians 9:20-21: "To the Jews I became as a Jew, in order to win Jews. To those under the law I became as one under the law (though not being myself under the law) that I might win those under the law. To those outside the law I became as one outside the law (not being outside the law of God but under the law of Christ) that I might win those outside the law." Paul is not

---

[333] John Reisinger helpfully writes, "First, even though the law, as codified covenant terms, has a historical beginning at Sinai, the underlying principles of all those laws, except the sabbath, were already revealed to man through the original creation. Neither knowledge of God and his character nor the reality of known sin began at Sinai. Secondly, even though the law, viewed as a covenant document, ended when Christ established the New Covenant, the unchanging ethical elements that underlie the commandments written on the tables of stone are just as binding on us today as they were on an Israelite," *Tablets of Stone*, 105. Gentry writes similarly, "What we can say to represent accurately the teaching of Scripture is that the righteousness of God codified, enshrined, and encapsulated in the old covenant has not changed and that this same righteousness is now codified and enshrined in the new," "The Covenant at Sinai," 60.

[334] Moo, "The Law of Christ as the Fulfillment of the Law of Moses," 368

under the Mosaic law, but he is under the law of God,
which is now the law of Christ. This is quite clear. The
natural law was once enshrined in the law of Moses, but
now is enshrined in the law of Christ. C.H. Dodd writes,

> I would suggest that the various forms of expression
> would be consistent with a conception of the 'law of God' as
> something wider and more inclusive than the 'law' *simpliciter*,
> in the sense of Torah. At one stage and on one level this law
> of God is presented by the Torah, and on that level a man's
> response to the Torah is, quite genuinely, a response to the
> law of God; ... At another stage and upon a different level the
> law of God may be mediated in some other, perhaps some
> more adequate form, in which it may be obeyed by one who
> is no longer subject to Torah...The law of God, which at one
> stage and on one level finds expression in the Torah, may at
> another stage and on a different level find expression in the
> 'law of Christ.'[335]

This natural law is eternally normative, as it reflects the
will and character of God. It consists of transcendent moral
principles.[336] We are only bound to those parts of the
Mosaic law which are part of natural law, which is
repeated in the law of Christ. As Luther puts it, "We will
regard Moses as a teacher, but we will not regard him as
our lawgiver-unless he agrees with both the New
Testament and the natural law...we are not to follow
[Moses] except so far as he agrees with the natural law.
Moses is a teacher and a doctor of the Jews. We have our

[335] Dodd, *More New Testament Studies,* 137.

[336] Schreiner, *40 Questions,* 104.

own master, Christ, and he has set before us what we are to
know, do, and leave undone."[337]

---

[337] Luther, "How Christians Should Regard Moses," 139, 147-48.
  Ethicist Michael Hill writes, "True, Christians are not under the old
  package called the 'Law', but the framework of creation that
  surrounds both packages provides for some continuity," The How
  and Why of Love, 188.

CONCLUSION

We live in a postmodern and pluralistic culture that eschews absolute truth. This has huge implications for the arena of morals. Christianity is at odds with ethical relativism, but it won't do to simply appeal to God's law. The crucial and complex question is: What is God's law? We have seen the Christian faith is not simply about ethics. The Christian faith is founded upon and centered upon the gospel of Jesus Christ. This good news is just that: *news*. It's an announcement outside of us about a victory that has been won. Christ was put to death and raised for sinners. We are declared right by having our sins forgiven through faith. Justification is the great indicative. Our obedience *flows from* this fact. Sanctification follows justification; the indicative is the foundation for the imperative.

We saw that new covenant believers are not under the Mosaic law. This does not mean that new covenant believers are without "law" though. We are still under the law of God, which for us is the law of Christ. I unpacked five aspects of the law of Christ. It is the law of love, the example of our Lord Jesus Christ, the teaching of Jesus, the teaching of the New Testament, and finally the whole canon interpreted in light of the Christ event. We concluded by showing that there is both continuity and discontinuity between the law of Christ and the law of Moses. Continuity is based on natural law, which is grounded in creation and expressed in both covenants.

May Christ's new covenant community be faithful in obeying him as we wait on our great God and King.

Soli Deo Gloria

BIBLIOGRAPHY

Adeyemi, Femi. "The New Covenant Law and the Law of Christ." *Bibliotheca Sacra* 163, no. 652 (October-December 2006): 438-52.

————. "What Is The New Covenant "Law" In Jeremiah 31:33?." *Bibliotheca Sacra* 163, no. 651 (July-September 2006): 312-21.

Arnold, Clinton E. "Returning to the Domain of the Powers: *Stoicheia* as Evil Spirits in Galatians 4:3, 9." *Novum Testamentum* 38, no. 1 (January 1996): 54-76.

Belleville, Linda L. "'Under Law': Structural Analysis and the Pauline Concept of Law in Galatians 3.21-4.11." *Journal for the Study of the New Testament* 26 (1986): 53-78.

Bird, Michael. *The Saving Righteousness of God*. Eugene, OR: Wipf & Stock Publishers, 2007.

Block, Daniel I. "My Servant David: Ancient Israel's Vision of the Messiah." In *Israel's Messiah in the Bible and The Dead Sea Scrolls*, ed. Richard S. Hess and M. Daniel Carroll R, 17-56. Grand Rapids: Baker Academic, 2003.

Blomberg, Craig L. *Matthew*. The New American Commentary. Nashville: Broadman Press, 1992.

————. "The Law in Luke-Acts." *Journal for the Study of the New Testament* 22 (October 1984): 53-80.

Calvin, John. *Commentaries on the Epistle of Paul the Apostle to the Romans*. Translated by John Owen. Grand Rapids: Baker Book House, 2005.

_____. *Commentaries on the Epistles of Paul to the Galatians and Ephesians*. Translated by William Pringle. Vol. 21 of *Calvin's Commentaries*. Grand Rapids, MI: Baker Books, 2005.

_____. *Institutes of the Christian Religion*. Edited by John T. McNeill. Translated by Ford Lewis Battles. Library of Christian Classics, vols. 20-21. Philadelphia: Westminster, 1960. Reissued, Louisville, KY: Westminster John Knox Press, 2006.

Carson, D.A. *The Cross and Christian Ministry*. Grand Rapids, MI: Baker Books, 1993.

_____. "Atonement in Romans 3:21-26," In *The Glory of the Atonement*, ed. Charles E. Hill and Frank A. James III, 119-39. Downers Grove, IL: InterVarsity Press, 2004.

_____. *The Gospel According to John*. The Pillar New Testament Commentary. Grand Rapids: Eerdmans, 1991.

_____. *The Sermon on the Mount*. Grand Rapids: Baker Book House, 1978.

_____. "The Vindication of Imputation." In *Justification in Perspective*. Edited by Bruce L. McCormack (Grand Rapids, MI: Baker Academic, 2006),46-78.

_____. *Matthew*. Vol. 1. In *The Expositor's Bible Commentary*. Edited by Frank E. Gaebelein. Grand Rapids, MI: Zondervan, 1995.

_____. "Reflections on Salvation and Justification in the New Testament." *Journal of the Evangelical Theological Society* 40, no. 4 (December 1997): 581-608.

_____. *Showing the Spirit*. Grand Rapids: Baker Books, 1987.

Cole, Graham A. *He Who Gives Life: The Doctrine of the Holy Spirit*. Wheaton, IL: Crossway Books, 2007.

Cranfield, C.E.B. *A Critical and Exegetical Commentary on the Epistle to the Romans.* Vol. 1. The International Critical Commentary. Edinburgh: T & T Clark, 1975.

Das, A. Andrew. *Paul and the Jews.* Peabody, MA: Hendrickson, 2003.

Deidun, T.J. *New Covenant Morality in Paul.* Rome: Biblical Institute Press, 1981.

Dodd, C.H. *More New Testament Studies.* Grand Rapids: Eerdmans, 1968.

Dorsey, David A. "The Law of Moses and the Christian: A Compromise." *Journal of the Evangelical Theological Society* 34, no. 3 (September 1991): 321-34.

Edwards, Jonathan. *The Works of Jonathan Edwards.* Peabody, MA: Hendrickson Publishers, 2003.

Fee, Gordon D. *The First Epistle to the Corinthians.* The New International Commentary on the New Testament. Grand Rapids: Eerdmans, 1987.

_____. *God's Empowering Presence: The Holy Spirit in the Letters of Paul.* Peabody, MA: Hendrickson Publishers, 1994.

_____. *Paul, the Spirit, and the People of God.* Peabody, MA: Hendrickson Publishers, 1996.

Ferguson, Sinclair B. *The Holy Spirit.* Downers Grove: InterVarsity Press, 1996.

The First London Confession of Faith. Belton, TX: Sovereign Grace Ministries, 2004.

Frame, John M. *Salvation Belongs to the Lord.* Phillipsburg, NJ: P&R Publishing, 2006.

Furnish, Victor Paul. *Theology and Ethics in Paul.* Nashville: Abingdon, 1968.

Gaffin Jr., Richard B. *By Faith, Not By Sight: Paul and the Order of Salvation*. Waynesboro, GA: Paternoster Press, 2006.

Gentry, Peter J. "The Covenant at Sinai." *The Southern Baptist Journal of Theology* 12, no. 3 (Fall 2008): 38-63.

Goldsworthy, Graeme. *Preaching the Whole Bible as Christian Scripture*. Grand Rapids: Eerdmans, 2000.

Hafemann, Scott J. *Second Corinthians*. The NIV Application Commentary. Grand Rapids: Zondervan, 2000.

Hagner, Donald A. "Paul & Judaism," In *Revisting Paul's Doctrine of Justification* by Peter Stuhlmacher. Downers Grove, IL: InterVarstity Press, 2001.

Harless, Hal. "The Cessation of the Mosaic Covenant." *Bibliotheca Sacra* 160 (July-September 2003): 349-66.

Harris, Murray J. *Slave of Christ: A New Testament Metaphor for Total Devotion to Christ*. Downers Grove, IL: Inter-Varsity Press, 1999.

Hays, Richard B. "Christology and Ethics in Galatians: The Law of Christ." *The Catholic Biblical Quarterly* 49, no. 1 (January 1987): 268-90.

Hill, Michael. *The How and Why of Love: An Introduction to Evangelical Ethics*. : Matthias Media, 2002.

Horton, Michael. *The Gospel-Driven Life*. Grand Rapids: Baker Books, 2009.

_____. *Christless Christianity*. Grand Rapids: Baker Books, 2008.

_____. *Introducing Covenant Theology*. Grand Rapids: Baker, 2006.

Kasemann, Ernst. *New Testament Questions for Today*. Philadelphia: Fortress Press, 1969.

Keller, Tim. *The Reason for God*. New York: Dutton, 2008.

Kirk, J.R. Daniel. "Conceptualising Fulfilment in Matthew." *Tyndale Bulletin* 59, no. 1 (2008): 77-98.

Kline, Meredith G. *The Structure of Biblical Authority*. Grand Rapids: Eerdmans, 1972.

Kruse, C.G. "Law." In *New Dictionary of Biblical Theology*. Edited by T. Desmond Alexander, et al, 629-36. Downers Grove, IL: InterVarsity Press, 2000.

Ladd, George Eldon. *A Theology of the New Testament*. Grand Rapids: Eerdmans, 1974.

Leiter, Charles. "The Law – Its Essence vs. Its Implications." Retrieved 25 November 2009 from http://www.todaysamericandream.com/TheLawCharlesLeiter.pdf.

Letham, Robert. *The Work of Christ*. Downers Grove: InterVarsity Press, 1993.

Lints, Richard. *The Fabric of Theology: A prolegomenon to Evangelical Theology*. Grand Rapids, MI: Eerdmans, 1993.

Long, Gary D. *Biblical Law and Ethics: Absolute and Covenantal*. Frederick, MD: New Covenant Media, 2008.

Longenecker, Richard N. *Galatians*. Word Biblical Commentary 41. Dallas: Word, 1990.

_____. "The Pedagogical Nature of the Law in Galatians 3:19-4:7." *Journal of the Evangelical Theological Society* 25.1 (March 1982): 53-61.

_____. *Paul: Apostle of Liberty*. New York: Harper and Row Publishers, 1964.

Lusk, Rich. "N.T. Wright and Reformed Theology: Friends or Foes." *Reformation and Revival Journal* 11, no. 2 (Spring 2002): 34-53.

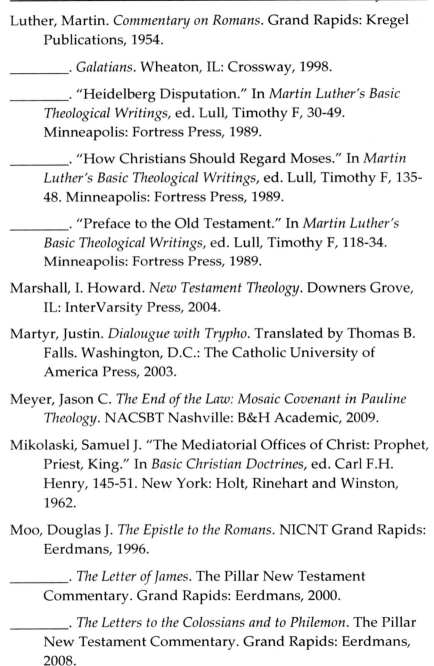

Luther, Martin. *Commentary on Romans.* Grand Rapids: Kregel Publications, 1954.

_____. *Galatians.* Wheaton, IL: Crossway, 1998.

_____. "Heidelberg Disputation." In *Martin Luther's Basic Theological Writings*, ed. Lull, Timothy F, 30-49. Minneapolis: Fortress Press, 1989.

_____. "How Christians Should Regard Moses." In *Martin Luther's Basic Theological Writings*, ed. Lull, Timothy F, 135-48. Minneapolis: Fortress Press, 1989.

_____. "Preface to the Old Testament." In *Martin Luther's Basic Theological Writings*, ed. Lull, Timothy F, 118-34. Minneapolis: Fortress Press, 1989.

Marshall, I. Howard. *New Testament Theology.* Downers Grove, IL: InterVarsity Press, 2004.

Martyr, Justin. *Dialougue with Trypho.* Translated by Thomas B. Falls. Washington, D.C.: The Catholic University of America Press, 2003.

Meyer, Jason C. *The End of the Law: Mosaic Covenant in Pauline Theology.* NACSBT Nashville: B&H Academic, 2009.

Mikolaski, Samuel J. "The Mediatorial Offices of Christ: Prophet, Priest, King." In *Basic Christian Doctrines*, ed. Carl F.H. Henry, 145-51. New York: Holt, Rinehart and Winston, 1962.

Moo, Douglas J. *The Epistle to the Romans.* NICNT Grand Rapids: Eerdmans, 1996.

_____. *The Letter of James.* The Pillar New Testament Commentary. Grand Rapids: Eerdmans, 2000.

_____. *The Letters to the Colossians and to Philemon.* The Pillar New Testament Commentary. Grand Rapids: Eerdmans, 2008.

_____. "The Law of Moses or the Law of Christ." In *Continuity and Discontinuity: Perspectives on the Relationship Between the Old and New Testaments*. Edited by John S. Feinberg, 203-18. Wheaton, IL: Crossway Books, 1988.

_____. "Jesus and the Authority of the Mosaic Law." *Journal for the Study of the New Testament* 20 (1984): 3-49.

_____. "Law." In *Dictionary of Jesus and the Gospels*, ed. Joel B. Green, Scot McKnight, and I. Howard Marshall, 450461. Downers Grove, IL: InterVarstity Press, 1992.

_____. "Paul and the Law in the Last Ten Years." *Scottish Journal of Theology* 40 (1987): 287-307.

_____. "The Law of Christ as the Fulfillment of the Law of Moses: A Modified Lutheran View." In *Five Views on Law and Gospel*, ed. Stanley N. Gundry, 319-76. Grand Rapids: Zondervan, 1999.

_____. "Law, Works of the Law, and Legalism in Paul." *Westminster Theological Journal* 45 (1983): 73-100.

Morris, Leon. *The Apostolic Preaching of the Cross*. Grand Rapids: Eerdmans, 1965.

Motyer, J. Alec. *The Prophecy of Isaiah*. Downers Grove, IL: InterVarsity Press, 1993.

Nelson, P.G. "Christian Morality: Jesus' Teaching on the Law." *Themelios* 32, no. 1 (October 2006): 4-17.

O'Brien, Peter T. *The Letter to the Ephesians*. The Pillar New Testament Commentary. Grand Rapids: Eerdmans, 1999.

Peterson, David G. *The Acts of the Apostles*. The Pillar New Testament Commentary. Grand Rapids: Eerdmans, 2009.

Peterson, David. *Engaging With God: A Biblical Theology of Worship*. Downers Grove, IL: InterVarstiy Press, 1992.

Piper, John. _The Future of Justification: A Response to N.T. Wright._ Wheaton, IL: Crossway Books, 2007.

_____. _The Justification of God: An Exegetical and Theological Study of Romans 9:1-23._ Grand Rapids: Baker Books, 1993.

_____. _Counted Righteous in Christ._ Wheaton, IL: Crossway Books, 2002.

Rainbow, Paul A. _The Way of Salvation: The Role of Christian Obedience in Justifications._ Waynesboro, GA: Paternoster Press, 2005.

Reid, D.G. "Elements/Elemental Spirits of the World." In _Dictionary of Paul and His Letters._ Edited by Gerald F. Hawthorne, et al, 229-233. Downers Grove, IL: InterVarsity Press, 1993.

Reisinger, John G. _But I Say Unto You._ Frederick, MD: New Covenant Media, 2006.

_____. _Tablets of Stone & the History of Redemption._ Frederick, MD: New Covenant Media, 2004.

Ridderbos, Herman N. _Redemptive History and the New Testament Scriptures._ Grand Rapids: Baker Book House, 1963.

_____. _Paul: An Outline of his Theology._ Grand Rapids: Eerdmans, 1975.

_____. _When the Time Had Fully Come._ Scarsdale, NY: Westminster Publishing House, 1982.

Rosner, B.S. "Biblical Theology." In _New Dictionary of Biblical Theology._ Edited by T. Desmond Alexander, et al, 3-11. Downers Grove, IL: InterVarsity Press, 2000.

Sanders, E.P. _Paul and Palestinian Judaism: A Comparison of Patterns of Religion._ Philadelphia: Fortress, 1977.

Schreiner, Thomas R. _The Law and Its Fulfillment: A Pauline Theology of Law._ Grand Rapids: Baker Books, 1993.

_____. *40 Questions About the Law*. Grand Rapids: Kregel Academic, forthcoming.

_____. "The Commands of God." In *Central Themes in Biblical Theology: Mapping Unity in Diversity*. Edited by Scott J. Hafemann and Paul R. House (Grand Rapids: Baker Academic, 2007), 66-101.

_____. *Galatians*. Zondervan Exegetical Commentary. Grand Rapids: Zondervan, forthcoming.

_____. *New Testament Theology*. Grand Rapids: Baker Academic, 2008.

_____. *Paul: Apostle of God's Glory in Christ*. Downers Grove, IL: IVP Academic, 2001.

_____. *Romans*. Baker Exegetical Commentary on the New Testament 6. Grand Rapids: Baker Academic, 1998.

Seifrid, Mark A. *Christ, Our Righteousness: Paul's Theology of Justification*. Downers Grove, IL: InterVarsity Press, 2000.

_____. "Righteousness Language in the Hebrew Scriptures and Early Judaism: Linguistic Considerations Critical to the Interpretation of Paul." In *Justification and Variegated Nomism, Volume 1: The Complexities of Second Temple Judaism*, eds. D.A. Carson, Peter T. O'Brien, and Mark A. Seifrid. Tubingen and Grand Rapids: Mohr Siebeck, 2001.

Sproul, R.C. *Getting the Gospel Right: The Tie That Binds Evangelicals Together*. Grand Rapids: Baker Books, 1998.

Stanton, Graham. "The Law of Christ: A Neglected Theological Gem?" In *Reading Texts, Seeking Wisdom*, ed. David F. Ford and Graham Stanton, 169-84. London: SCM Press, 2003.

_____. "The Law of Moses and the Law of Christ." In *Paul and the Mosaic Law*, ed., James D.G Dunn, 99-116. Grand Rapids: Eerdmans, 1996.

Stuhlmacher, Peter. *Revisiting Paul's Doctrine of Justification*. Downers Grove, IL: InterVarsity Press, 2001.

Thielman, Frank. *The Law and the New Testament: The Question of Continuity*. New York: The Crossroad Publishing Company, 1999.

_____. "Law and Liberty in the Ethics of Paul." *Ex Auditu* 11 (1995): 63-75.

_____. *Paul & the Law: A Contextual Approach*. Downers Grove, IL: InterVarsity Press, 1994.

_____. *Theology of the New Testament*. Grand Rapids: Zondervan, 2005.

Tripp, Paul David. *A Quest for More*. Greensboro, NC: New Growth Press, 2007.

Turner, Max. *The Holy Spirit and Spiritual Gifts*. Peabody, MA: Hendrickson Publishers, 1996.

Venema, Cornelis P. *Getting the Gospel Right: Assessing the Reformation and New Perspectives on Paul*. Carlisle, PA: The Banner of Truth Trust, 2006.

Verbrugge, Verlyn D., ed. *New Internatilan Dictionary of New Testament Theology: Abridged Edition*. Grand Rapids: Zondervan, 2000.

Vickers, Brian. *Jesus' Blood and Righteousness*. Wheaton, IL: Crossway, 2006.

Vos, Geerhardus. *The Pauline Eschatology*. Phillipsburg, NJ: P&R Publishing, 1994.

Webb, Barry G. *The Message of Isaiah*. The Bible Speaks Today. Downers Grove, IL: InterVarsity Press, 1996.

Weima, Jeffrey A.D. "1-2 Thessalonians." In *Commentary on the New Testament Use of the Old Testament*, ed. G.K. Beale and D.A. Carson, 871-889. Grand Rapids: Baker Academic, 2007.

Wells, Tom and Fred Zaspel. *New Covenant Theology*. Frederick, MD: New Covenant Media, 2002.

Wells, Tom. *The Priority of Jesus Christ*. Frederick, MD: New Covenant Media, 2005.

Wenham, David. *Paul: Follower of Jesus or Founder of Christianity*. Grand Rapids: Eerdmans, 1995.

Wenham, John. *Christ and the Bible*. Grand Rapids: Baker Books, 1994.

Westerholm, Stephen. *Israel's Law and the Church's Faith*. Grand Rapids: Eerdmans, 1988.

_____. "Law and Gospel in Jesus and Paul." In *Jesus and Paul Reconnected: Fresh Pathways into an Old Debate*, ed. Todd D. Still, 19-36. Grand Rapids: Eerdmans, 2007.

_____. "Letter and Spirit: The Foundation of Pauline Ethics." *New Testament Studies* 30 (1984): 229-48.

_____. *Perspectives Old and New on Paul: The "Lutheran" Paul and His Critics*. Grand Rapids: Eerdmans, 2004.

_____. "On Fulfilling the Whole Law (Gal. 5:14)." *Svensk exegetisk årsbok* 51-52 (1986-87): 229-37.

_____. "The Law and the 'Just Man' (1 Tim 1,3-11)." *Studia Theologica* 36 (1982): 79-95.

_____. "The Law in the Sermon on the Mount." *Criswell Theological Review* 6, no. 1 (Fall 1992): 43-56.

The Westminster Confession of Faith. Atlanta: Committee for Christian Education & Publications, 1990.

White, A. Blake. *The Newness of the New Covenant*. Frederick, MD: New Covenant Media, 2008.

Williams, Sam K. "The "Righteousness of God" in Romans." *Journal of Biblical Literature* 99, no. 2 (1980): 241-90.

Wilson, Todd A. "The Law of Christ and the Law of Moses: Reflections on a Recent Trend in Interpretation." *Currents in Biblical Research* 5, no. 1 (October 2006): 123-44.

Wright, N.T. *The Last Word: Scripture and the Authority of God-Getting Beyond the Bible Wars.* New York: HarperOne, 2005.

_____. *The New Testament and the People of God.* Christian Origins and the People of God: Volume 1. Minneapolis: Fortress Press, 1992.

_____. *Jesus and the Victory of God.* Minneapolis: Fortress Press, 1996.

_____. *What Saint Paul Really Said.* Grand Rapids: Eerdmans, 1997.

Zaspel, Fred G. "The Apostolic Model for Christian Ministry: An Analysis of 1 Corinthians 2:1-5." *Reformation & Revival* 7, no. 1 (Winter 1998): 20-34.

CPSIA information can be obtained at www.ICGtesting.com
Printed in the USA
BVOW04s1407080914

365912BV00030B/641/P